The Imitation of Christ

The Imitation of Christ

Thomas à Kempis

Translated by E. M. Blaiklock

Foreword by J. John

HODDER

First published in Great Britain in 1979

This edition published in Great Britain in 2009 by Hodder & Stoughton
An Hachette UK company

3

A CIP catalogue record for this title is available from the British Library

ISBN 978 0 340 98016 3

Typeset in Celeste by Hewer Text UK Ltd, Edinburgh
Printed and bound in the UK by CPI Mackays, Chatham ME5 8TD

Hodder & Stoughton policy is to use papers that are natural, renewable
and recyclable products and made from wood grown in sustainable
forests. The logging and manufacturing processes are expected to
conform to the environmental regulations of the country of origin.

Hodder & Stoughton Ltd
338 Euston Road
London NW1 3BH

www.hodderfaith.com

Contents

Foreword

Every man and woman on this earth longs to have a really good life. We yearn to find peace, love, happiness, adventure and contentment. Jesus says that he came to give us this kind of life. He said, 'I have come that they may have life, and have it to the full', and that 'your joy may be complete'. Jesus said, in reference to himself, 'I am the way and the truth and the life.' When we hear these words of Jesus we shout, 'Amen! I will have some of that!'

And yet, even as Christians who are seeking to follow Jesus, as we go about our daily lives we often find ourselves perplexed and asking God, 'What is your will for my life? What are you trying to say to me? What do you want me to do in this situation? Am I hearing you clearly, Lord? Why is this or that happening to me? Are you with me, Lord? I want to grow closer to you, can you show me how?'

In the midst of this quest for God, we are super-busy and bombarded with more information than any generation in human history. Moment by moment, we are stretched by people and things competing for our attention. With the Internet and mobile phones, we can be reached anytime, anywhere. Even more, the average Westerner is said to see 1,400 advertisements a day asking us to buy the best new gadget to bring us happiness.

All of us living in this crazy, fast-paced world – including Christians – could use some advice and wisdom on how to navigate the spiritual life and to hear God. In his timeless classic, *The Imitation of Christ*, Thomas à Kempis has given us a treasure chest of how to draw close to Jesus Christ. This book has changed the lives of thousands of followers of Jesus over the centuries. It has not only had an impact on saints, it has drawn the hearts and minds of ordinary, everyday Christians to go deeper with God. We have so much to learn from this fifteenth-century monk, who was known as a man of deep prayer and closeness to Jesus, and who even copied the Bible by hand at least four times!

Born in Germany at around 1380, Thomas à Kempis grew up during times of great trial in the world and in the Church. Disease, wars, corruption and ecclesiastical battles – between multiple people claiming to be Pope – ravaged society. It was not in any way a quiet, peaceful existence. Life for people in the early 1400s was filled with immense stress and strain. It is no wonder that Thomas was drawn to the spiritual life as a young man through an encounter with The Brethren of the Common Life, a group of people who followed the Christian teacher Gerard Groote. His mentor Groote sought to live life like the early Christians and led a movement called Modern Devotion, which rejected worldly pretension and embraced a holy life.

During his quest for God, Thomas attended school and received an education, but he soon found himself desiring quiet and solitude. In 1406, Thomas followed his brother, John, and became a monk at the Mount Saint Agnes monastery. He was ordained priest in 1413 and was made sub-prior of the monastery in 1429. It was during his time at the monastery that he gave the world one of the best known Christian books on devotion. Next to the Bible, *The Imitation of Christ* is the most widely read spiritual work of all time!

What makes this book such a gem to the Christian reader? The simple answer is that it is the work (through immersion in prayer, Scripture and the sacraments) of a man who found the secret of growing closer to God in a challenging world. In *The Imitation of Christ*, Thomas not only provides practical insights and methods for living a full life in Christ, he also models it for us.

The Imitation of Christ is divided into four books. The first, 'Counsels Useful for Spiritual Living', reads like a brilliant stream of proverbs and wise words. It is wisdom literature at its best, and begins with a call to imitate and follow Christ and to despise all the vanities of the world. Thomas notes that the truth found in the Gospels of Christ will be 'hidden manna' for the one who follows them. He argues, though, that one must reject the pulls of the world in order to follow Christ, and gives a strong warning to reject worldly vanity and the pride that stems from intellectual pursuit, vain secular study, materialism, misconceived self-understanding and power. Instead, Thomas calls on the follower of Jesus to seek God and God alone in a spirit of total humility and depravity, knowing that we are sinful creatures in need of God's grace and assistance.

> Do not depend on yourself, but establish your hope in God. Do what is in your power, and God will be with your good will. Trust not in your own knowledge, nor in the cleverness of anyone alive, but rather in the grace of God who helps the humble, and brings low those who presume upon themselves.
>
> Boast not in riches if you have them, nor in friends because they are powerful, but in God who provides all things, and above all things longs to give himself.

Thomas reminds us time and again that we should have a healthy fear of God, and that everything in this world should be lived in preparation for meeting God in judgment and eternal life:

> Keep yourself as a pilgrim and stranger upon earth, who has no concern with the business of the world. Keep your heart free and lifted up to God because you have not here 'a continuing city'. To him direct your prayers and daily groanings with tears, that your spirit may deserve after death to pass happily to God.

His words are sobering and at times jolting; however, he never forgets to highlight the comfort and abundant life that comes in following Christ. For to deny oneself is truly to find freedom, peace and perfect love.

Book Two, 'Advice About the Inner Life', continues many of the same themes of the first book, calling on Christians to turn to God and reject worldly ways.

> 'The Kingdom of God is within you,' says the Lord. Turn with your whole heart to God, and abandon this wretched world, and your soul will find peace. Learn to despise that which is without, and give yourself to that which is within, and you will see the kingdom of God come in you. For the kingdom of God is peace and joy in the Holy Spirit, which is not given to the godless – Christ will come to you, revealing his own consolation, if you have prepared for him a dwelling-place. All his glory and beauty is within, and there he is pleased to dwell. His visits are many to the inner man, sweet discourse, gracious consolation, great peace, and fellowship most marvellous.

Book Two especially talks about this wondrous dwelling of God in our hearts through even the toughest of trials. Thomas encourages us to glory in our daily crosses and the trials of this life.

Why therefore do you fear to take up the cross, through which is the road to the kingdom? In the cross is salvation, in the cross life, in the cross protection from our foes; in the cross is the inflow of heaven's sweetness, in the cross strength of mind, in the cross joy of the spirit; in the cross is the height of virtue, in the cross perfection of holiness. There is no salvation for the soul, nor hope of eternal life, save in the cross . . . If you willingly carry the cross, it will carry you and lead you to your desired haven, where assuredly will be the end of suffering, although that will not be here.

Book Three, 'On Consolation Within', shows the fruit of following the practical wisdom found in the first two books, and is written as a dialogue between Thomas and Jesus himself. It reads like a beautiful conversation between the most intimate lovers and friends, and proves that we truly can grow close to Jesus Christ and actually converse with him and be consoled and loved by him in ways beyond anything we could ask or imagine. Book Three illustrates the depth of love Jesus has for each and every person. Here we get a glimpse of how we can come to Jesus with all our hurts, fears, hopes, praise, gratitude, angers, frustrations and dreams and how Jesus responds with great care and direction. Thomas begins this book with these words:

'I will hearken to what the Lord God says within me.'
Blessed the soul which hears the Lord speaking within, and receives the word of consolation from his lips . . . These things says your beloved: 'I am your salvation, your peace and your life. Keep by me and you will find peace.'

The Imitation of Christ finally ascends to what Thomas sees as God's greatest gift – the Blessed Sacrament. Book

Four: 'On the Sacrament of the Altar' discusses Holy Communion. The Church teaches that a sacrament is an outward sign of an inward grace, and in this last section Thomas relishes this divine inward grace, given by God to humanity. In today's Christian culture, we can easily forget the gift God has given us in Holy Communion, but Thomas sees it as God's primary way of restoring us in a way that we could not do in our own strength. He writes, echoing the words of Jesus.

> 'Come to me all who labour and are heavy-laden and I will refresh you,' says the Lord. 'The bread which I shall give is my flesh, for the life of the world. Take it and eat, this is my Body, which is surrendered for you. Do this in memory of me. He who eats my flesh and drinks my blood, abides in me and I in him. The words which I have spoken to you are spirit and life.'

He rejoices in this holy, mysterious gift of Jesus: 'In this Sacrament spiritual grace is conferred, and lost virtue made good in the soul, and beauty marred by sin returns.' Thomas' writing on the Blessed Sacrament encourages all Christians to partake of this gift of God and to focus on the reality of being nourished by God himself.

Fellow Christian, I commend *The Imitation of Christ* to you. It remains as relevant today as it was over six hundred years ago. After reading this gift to us, may we say, with Thomas à Kempis, 'There is no journeying without a way, no knowing without truth, no living without life.' Read this treasure.

—*J. John (Canon), 2009*

Introduction

The Book

There are few books which have been read more assiduously during the last five centuries, than a small volume containing something less than 50,000 words of Latin, called the *Imitation of Christ*, traditionally by one Thomas à Kempis. It is a book which has spoken to the centuries and all manner of men. Pope John Paul I was reading it, according to report, when, on September 29 of 1978, he passed quietly to rest in bed, after his thirty-three days. It has been translated, it is said, into more languages than any other book, other than the Bible itself. It was a large and magnificently leathered tome, a French translation in my own library, which prompted, as August ended, a request for a translation. Looking for the Latin in response, I found I had two copies, a tiny vest-pocket edition from Paris in 1858, with a florid Latin introduction on the author's life, and a German edition, also with a Latin introduction, which is much concerned (how typically German!) with controversy over authorship. It was printed in Leipzig in 1847. Rummaging further, I found that I also possessed the Rev. William Benham's rather old-world English translation. In fact, English renderings date back to the century of its writing, and of the book itself some two thousand editions have appeared.

Christian man has, in a word, taken the Augustinian monk to his heart, even among the far from orthodox. I found, in that afternoon's preparatory browsings, an article, slipped inside the cover, after a habit of mine, of Benham's translation. It was by Frank Swinnerton, over the signature of 'John O'London', in that lamented weekly of the name. He had discovered Thomas à Kempis, and strangely enough through George Eliot, whose sombre novel, *The Mill on the Floss* was published in 1860 . . .

Maggie Tulliver, conscious more deeply of her lonely joylessness, as people sometimes are when spring grows green around their troubles, turned for consolation to books, Scott, Byron, and others. No dream-world, she found, could give her satisfaction. She wanted reality, but reality, hard and harsh, explained. Then she came upon a small, old clumsy volume, marked with ink turned rusty with the years. Following the underscored passages she felt a thrill of awe, 'as if she had been wakened in the night by a strain of solemn music telling of beings whose souls had been astir while hers was in a stupor'. Thomas à Kempis' voice came from the Middle Ages to Maggie Tulliver (alias George Eliot, surely?) as 'an unquestioned message'.

John Paul I, George Eliot, I myself (for I shall add a testimony), a varied and unequal trio are we, but representative of a multitude, who may not follow the old ascetic's footsteps far or everywhere, but find his mystic's message strangely moving. Miss Rita Snowden tells me I can add three more names: Edith Cavell and Dietrich Bonhoeffer had the *Imitation* in their cells the night before they died. It was the only book in Dag Hammerskjöld's case when he died . . . It will be much read again, thanks to that September night in the Vatican, and some who read may discover Jesus Christ afresh.

The Man

Who was Thomas? Thomas Haemmerline, was named Kempis from his native town of Kempen on the Rhine, north of Cologne. He was educated by the Brothers of the Common Life, and joined their association, a group devoted to fostering, in an age of much corruption, a loftier level of Christian life and devotion. Geert de Groote, whose life Thomas was to write, had gathered this band together a century before, but demanded no vows, and left his disciples free, cleric or lay, to pursue their ordinary vocations. They founded free schools in the Netherlands and in Germany, promoted copying and printing, and challenged laymen and priests alike with their lofty spirituality.

At twenty-two years of age, however, Thomas Haemmerline joined the community of Mount Saint Agnes, a monastery of the Augustinian Canons, in the diocese of Utrecht. There he lived for seventy years, until his death on July 26, 1471. It was a long life of copying, reading, and monastic prayer and piety.

Did he write the *Imitation of Christ*? To be sure, the work is such a mosaic of ideas and phrases from the Bible and more than one earlier mystic source, that it was inevitable that pedantry, or even scholarship, would challenge authorship.

The fact that the book was first put into circulation anonymously (about 1418), perhaps invited speculation. It was early assigned to Thomas à Kempis, and a Brussels manuscript actually bears his signature. Controversy dates back three centuries. Was it Saint Bonaventura, the Franciscan 'doctor seraphicus', who lived two centuries earlier than Thomas? Was it Jean de Gerson, the formidable 'doctor christianissimus', partly Thomas' contemporary? Or could it have been Innocent the Third, who marked the apex of the medieval Papacy, and who died in 1216?

Such challenges to tradition commonly, before the emergence of the German Ph.D. degree, were a mark of too much lucubration, and are certainly not worth vehement discussion. Frank Swinnerton, coming, he confesses, inexpertly on the controversy, wonders at the diligence of Samuel Kettlewell, a century ago, who devoted three large volumes and a multitude of words, to prove, 'by stupefaction if not by conviction', that Thomas did indeed write his book. Scarcely forty years ago, more briefly than the Reverend Kettlewell, one Doctor Douglas Gordon Barron, with fewer words but equal dogmatism, gave the authorship to the Frenchman of extraordinary scholarship, Jean de Gerson, already listed. He dismisses Thomas with unbecoming contempt. He was, he says, 'steeped in the Mariolatry of his time . . . Resting thereupon his trust in a divine beneficence, what knew à Kempis of that personal approach to God, that oneness with God which the *Imitation* proclaims to all who seek its guidance?'

Such an argument is hollow in the extreme. Because Thomas mentions the Madonna only once, he could not have written the book attributed to him! But there is no need to enter further into such controversy, save to remark, perhaps a little provocatively, that it is too often the young, the prejudiced, and the seekers after academic repute, who most vehemently attack tradition. A lifetime in classical and biblical literary criticism has made me careful to respect tradition, and not to abandon what long centuries have handed down, without the most weighty and documented evidence.

Suffice it, then, in conclusion, to say, that no convincing case has been made against the traditional authorship. Something more than sound and fury will be necessary to take the honour from the gentle and anxious Augustinian who looks from the pages of the *Imitation of Christ* – Mr. Fearing, perhaps, but a good man to know.

The Theme

If one theme can be disengaged from the book, one which shows its worth, and touches its occasional faultiness, it is humility. In humility towards God and man lies, Thomas believes, the secret of all excellence. It appears with the first pages. 'It is great wisdom and maturity to think nothing of ourselves, and to think always well and highly of others'. . . . 'Who hinders and troubles you more than the affections of your own heart, which you have not put to death?' . . . 'The more humble a man is in himself, and the more subject to God, so much the wiser will he be in all his affairs, and enjoy peace and quiet of heart' . . .

The book passes on to elaborate the theme in the form of mystic dialogues, rising somewhat above common reach, and comes to its climax in perhaps a disproportionate pre-occupation with the Sacrament of Communion, Book Four, which could have been omitted.

But it could be well to look more closely at humility as a disciplined Christianity sees it, because some disagreement with the *Imitation* could take shape here, and mar other worth. Humility is a noble word and the world needs more of that most basic virtue, for, truly, just as pride, the assertion of self, lies beneath or penetrates every vice, so humility is the solid foundation of all the virtues. Confucius said that, and gave the Red Guards one motive for burning his books. Christ professed it in all he did. It was a mark of Socrates.

Humility is complete absence of pride. It is emancipation from oneself, freedom from the base urge to boast, strut, pose. It is a correct estimate of oneself, an estimate which neither degrades nor exalts. Humble Albert Einstein, one of the great minds of the century, once said: 'The contrast between the popular estimate of my power and achievements and the reality is simply grotesque.'

The first and surest test of all greatness, in scholarship, art, science or any other sphere of excellence, is the absence of noisy self-assertion.

Humility does not hold the floor. The true scholar is seen to be completely free of that self-conscious academic vice which is always ready with the angled question or the subtly barbed remark, designed to show another's ignorance or disadvantage. Humility needs no shield or drawn sword. It is not in any way self-conscious. That is humility's inner quality. It does not need weapons. It is worn unconsciously like good health. It is, in fact, good health, health of mind and spirit, freed from the fear of being toppled from some posture, for postures are not manifest, a spirit without the need to protect itself from too close a scrutiny.

And so it is that the truly humble person is not thinking of himself. He can listen to others, and be the richer for not speaking. He may pity the arrogant, but he will feel for them, rather than be hurt by them.

One can be conscious of some virtues, know that one is honest, truthful, self-controlled, for some virtues are kept by a stern vigilance and a firm standing on guard. Humility is a stance and habit of the soul, which does not know itself.

Do we thus perhaps put a finger on a fault of Thomas' conception of humility? It is too self-conscious, sometimes too exhibitionist, too open to the caricature of the watching world. For all good is misrepresented deliberately by the bad, and that is why humility has too often been misrepresented as an abject, weak and self-despising spirit, unworthy of a self-respecting man. . . . 'Thank you, Master Copperfield, I'm sure it is very kind of you to make the offer but I am much too 'umble to accept it. I am greatly obliged, and I should like it of all things, but I am far too 'umble. There are people enough to tread on me in my lowly state without my doing outrage to their feelings by possessing learning. A person like myself should not aspire. If he is to get on in life he must get on 'umbly, Master Copperfield.'

Uriah's grovelling was, of course, not humility but a nicely contrived caricature. All virtues are subject to base imitation.

Epaminondas, the great fourth-century Theban general, was therefore merely an exhibitionist in the story Plutarch tells. He was seen, the day after a public triumph, going about with drooping head. Asked why, he replied: 'Yesterday I felt myself transported with vainglory, therefore I chastise myself today.'

He had a perfect right to enjoy, as we all sometimes do, an acclamation. If he sensed a whiff of unworthy pride, it was a matter for private therapy. Perhaps he had not seen the calm face of the bronze charioteer at Delphi.

Bear all this in mind, then, in reading this old book of devotion, but without impatience, remembering the world in which it was written, the gloom of the times, and even the wider understanding of the Lord himself which five centuries of experience, and an open Bible have conferred – to our deeper responsibility, as well as to our clearer understanding.

The Religion

Thomas à Kempis was a mystic, and in mysticism is contained both his merits and his faults, if his over-emphases deserve that term. Mysticism explains his sometimes painful striving for conscious union with God, his species of 'death-wish', his withdrawal from the world, his revulsion from sin. Mysticism, of course, must in some degree be part of all personal experience of Christ, all reaching-out of faith. Any careful description of mysticism would need, in fact, to begin with Paul and John, and pass on through history with attention to medieval hagiography, Wesleyan 'holiness', and the 'victorious living' of the so-called 'Keswick teaching'. But there is no movement of the spirit through all history, which has not been marked by its extravagances, born of man's proneness to extremes. And this, perhaps, in human experience is the process by which truth advances.

Mysticism is alive and included in all Christian living, and that is why so much of the *Imitation* is not as remote from modern orthodoxy and conservative Christianity as might have been supposed. Consider our traditional congregational hymns. Thomas would have revelled in John Newton's 'Amazing Grace', especially the last verse, in J. S. B. Monsell's 'O, worship the Lord in the beauty of holiness', and in Isaac Watts' 'Come, dearest Lord'. He would have sung with complete acceptance a hymn from a contemporary collection which boldly says:

> *I have given up all for Jesus,*
> *This vain world is nought to me,*
> *All its pleasures are forgotten,*
> *In remembering Calvary.*

One would hope that the car park would not be visible through the stained-glass window! 'Ten thousand times ten thousand', and the unwise 'Keswick' hymn 'Lower still lower . . .' touch his chief otherworldly preoccupations . . .

But consider such preoccupations in the light of the century in which his religious thought took shape. Life could be 'brutish and short'. The fifteenth century was hardly aware that the dawn wind was blowing, and the New Learning preparing the way for the awakening of the human spirit which we call the Renaissance. Europe was emerging from the chaos which marked the end of the Middle Ages, but it was a grim time in which to live, with mankind at large shortlived, sickness-ridden, starved, cold and in the dark. The few, the rich and the lucky had shelter, some degree of warmth, food, albeit of small variety, but even the highest lacked the vast advantages of maturer medicine, surgery, dentistry, optometry, and the thousand amenities, which a century of affluence, and harsh nature tamed, takes too readily for granted. Evil was as arrogantly abroad, as naked and ugly as it fast becomes again.

To long for escape from it all, for paradise and rest among the 'ten thousand times ten thousand' who 'throng up the streets of light' was a natural-enough longing. And was it not, too, a stronger urge to hold the feeble body in contempt, when that mortal thing was so visibly and early marked and marred by the evidence of its transience? Thomas à Kempis, surviving ninety-two years, must have been by far the oldest man in Europe, his generation long since decimated and swept off in the insanitary cities of a plague-ridden century. They lived intimately with death, a situation prolonged into Victorian times. Such ages come to terms with death.

Nor, indeed, when shattering bereavement, personal catastrophe, or even the inevitable ills of advanced years befall, can modern Christians deny that the old longing 'to depart and be with Christ, something far better', gains daily in appeal. It is only recently that large numbers have been able with some success to thrust death aside, or live long enough to weary of continued life. And in the more sombre wards of many a hospital, there are those whose still-active mind is aware of the vast dichotomy, and finds the body a sad impediment. Thomas' words then seem less life-denying.

It is when such life-denying becomes a facet of humility that one must part company with our Augustinian. Self – our person's totality, must be commanded and controlled, but not despised and crushed. The indwelling Spirit of God works to enhance and beautify the person of its host. Sin, held in the heart's core, corrodes, eats away its host, destroys him. Christ, entertained in mystic union, makes surrendered man more truly alive, more truly the unique being he was born to be. He came 'that we might have life and have it more abundantly'. Thomas, and those among us who so similarly err, is at fault when he longs to be 'nothing, nothing' as another contemporary hymn has it. We seek no Nirvana, but Heaven which is here as well as there, a place of quickened life, a foreglimpse of that which shall so richly be.

A Personal Word

It is perhaps relevant to speak personally. The present translation was a task begun just before Albino Luciani became Pope John Paul, whose death, thirty-three days later, added a few touching lines to the long story of Thomas à Kempis' *De Imitatione Christi*. Over that month of September in all spare time available, I had pressed on with the translation, no task of great difficulty with Latin so simple. The work was three-quarters finished when John Paul died, and the world learned that *De Imitatione Christi* was his book of evening devotions.

It is pertinent to ask: What impact had this book, mediaeval, mystical, now almost five-and-a-half centuries old, on the mind of an academic Christian, an 'informed Conservative', if you will, today? I simply answer that I found it challenging, found the words, as I wrote them down, sometimes cohering into prayer, and discovering, after a long evening with it, sentences of Latin mingling with my devotions. I could touch a hand in fellowship across the centuries.

Thomas' view of Holy Communion, in the tradition of his church, was a little remote from mine. But how could a reader, properly desiring to 'eat and drink worthily', be other than daunted by the soul-searching and self-examination, the zeal for uprightness and abandonment to God, which this austere and single-minded man brought to the handling of divine and mystic symbols?

I may deplore those traits already mentioned, his lack of evangelism or even social action, the introversion of Brother Thomas' faith, and his too anxious preoccupation with his personal salvation, the uneasiness before the justice of God the Father, and God's judgment, alongside the adoration of Christ, the Son. I may dislike the view of humility which seems at times to seek that Buddhist nothingness, and an abasement which almost appears to destroy the 'new man' in a zealous passion to put the 'old man' to death.

But all this frankly said, it remains true that Paul told the folk of Philippi to 'work out salvation with reverence and self-distrust', and our own soul's culture must not be lost in busy rushing to and fro, in 'the earthquake, wind and fire', as Elijah learned. And for all the access and the freedom which we have in Christ, and for all the sound theology in that hymn of Wesley, I am surely not the only one to sense a trace of arrogance when I sing:

> *Bold I approach the eternal throne*
> *And claim the crown through Christ my own.*

If God would not have us 'lie on the floor of the world, with the seven sins for rods', as Chesterton phrases it, to stride the floor of heaven with a too unmuted tread is perhaps not quite befitting.

The little book (it is quite a deal less than half the size of the New Testament) is subduing. I could wish Thomas was less hard on laughter, less fearful of a simple chat, less contemptuous of himself, with a 'better self-image', if you must have the phrase . . . but grant all this, and his standards of holiness could well be transplanted, his patience 'under the mighty hand of God', could well be that of all who suffer, his self-effacement, for all its exaggeration, deserves a second look in these too self-assertive days, and his love for Christ is a joy we should regain though expressed, perhaps, in language less lush and mystical. In short, I am the better for reading him, more deeply challenged to deal with that which mars the life, sterner with myself, more sensitive to holiness for having lived with Thomas à Kempis' Latin book for these six weeks.

The Translation

A word, in conclusion, on this attempt to 'English' him. Thomas, of course, writes in the Vulgate tradition, with those innovations of syntax which Jerome's Latin acquires from the Greek New Testament, the substantival infinitive, for example, and indirect statement in a clause like Greek. Apart from such minimal departures from the norm, the Latin is strong and simple, a fine medium of communication, as the Church, and the scholars of many centuries, showed. It is ecclesiastical Latin at its best.

Thomas makes little attempt at 'fine writing'. He might have regarded such an endeavour as impious, and lacking in humility. He wrote to be understood and his enduring popularity is testimony to his great success. How well-trained he was in Classical Latin is difficult to assess. If a moment is spared to check an unusual word in Lewis and Short, it is frequently to be found that the dictionary dubs it 'rare but classical'. Of the Ciceronian period there is little trace. Anyone who reads Latin as Latin, without mentally translating (a diminishing tribe, alas!), knows the rhetorical tension of the Ciceronian period, moving on to the final verbal construction which locks the whole system into rounded meaning. It is a great feat of language.

Occasionally, one is conscious that Thomas is seeking something like the same effect, but not so much by a periodic structure, as by a piling of phrase on phrase, or clause on clause, each repetition reinforcing and varying the theme, and holding the attention to the end. Perhaps Hebrew parallelism lies behind it. The writer knew the Psalms intimately. The result, in Latin and English, is a sentence more effective in spoken than in written form.

I have made no attempt to break such rhetorical paragraphs down. It is not a translator's task to eliminate even wearisome and involved features of his author's style. The translator has not even the right to try to improve the style of the original. He must allow the right to speak even to the point of retaining a piece of awkwardness. The translator is not a commentator. He will rather reproduce an obscurity than tamper with a meaning.

One small difficulty cannot be avoided. If one knew how, where and from whom young Thomas Haemmerline learned his Latin, it might just be possible to know how much of the significance of some Classical Latin words remains in this ecclesiastical language of the fifteenth century. Does 'securitas', for example, mean 'security' or, as it did in Classical Latin, 'freedom from care'? Does 'desiderium' mean 'desire' or, more strongly, 'longing'? Does 'vilis' mean 'cheap' or 'vile'? I have taken the liberty of allowing the context to decide the issue, and in general, with Latin abstracts, tried to avoid the misleading English derivative. It is too often a shade, or more than a shade removed from the Latin meaning. I can only hope that I have had some success in carrying to English readers the same impression which Thomas' Latin carried to those who could read him, in his day. Simplicity, a little stiffness, much repetition mark him. Sometimes, in a neat 'sententia' (surely a mark of some Silver Latin reading

– Seneca, perhaps?), he is memorable, and merits almost a column in the *Oxford Dictionary of Quotations*. Seneca? He quotes Seneca on the effect of crowds on the spirit. He knew perfectly well that he was quoting Seneca but, as queasy as Augustine was over Cicero, he says: 'Someone has said . . .'

But to return to the minor problems of translation. There are one or two terms, almost 'technical' in a religious sense. How, for example, should one render 'compunctio'? In one of the 'sententiae' listed on *ODQ*, Thomas says: 'Opto magis sentire compunctionem quam scire eius definitionem'. To render (*ODQ*): 'I had rather feel compunction than know its definition', is intolerably lame. Remembering that 'punctum' is a 'stab' or 'prick', I have risked, etymologically: 'I would rather feel the sting of conscience than define the term.' And what shall we say of 'perfectus'? Surely not 'perfect', since the comparative, 'perfectior', 'more perfect' is illogically used. I have tried, here and there, 'mature', but am conscious that the word sounds like another jargon, that of books on Christian living, ethics, psychology which, sometimes usefully, sometimes irritatingly, use the term today.

Conclusion

Here then the product. I have tried to let the author speak as he spoke. If the meaning eludes, the fault could be mine, as it could equally be his. For envoi and dedication, let it be: 'For all in Christ', for the little book bestrides all ecclesiastical divisions, as it crosses all the centuries, by-passes Renaissance and Reformation, and speaks to princes of the Church as it speaks to commoners.

– E. M. Blaiklock
October 16, 1978
Titirangi, Auckland, New Zealand

BOOK ONE

Counsels Useful for Spiritual Living

ONE

On the Imitation of Christ and Contempt for all the World's Vanities

1. 'He who follows me does not walk in darkness,' says the Lord. These are the words of Christ by which we are advised to imitate his life and ways, if we desire truly to be enlightened and to be freed from all blindness of the heart. Let it therefore be our chief preoccupation to think upon the life of Jesus Christ.

2. The teaching of Christ surpasses all the teaching of holy men, and he who has Christ's spirit will find there 'the hidden manna'. But it happens that many, from frequent hearing of the Gospel, are conscious of little longing for it, because they have not the spirit of Christ. But he who wishes fully and with relish to know the words of Christ, must be zealous to bring his whole life into conformity with him.

3. What does it profit you to argue profoundly about the Trinity, if you lack humility, and so displease the Trinity? Truly, deep words do not make a holy man and just. It is a virtuous life that makes a man dear to God. I would rather feel contrition than define the word. If you know the whole Bible superficially, and the words of all philosophers, what would all this profit you without the grace of God? 'Vanity of

vanities, all is vanity', save to love God and serve him alone. This is the highest wisdom, despising the world, to reach for the Kingdom of Heaven.

4. It is vanity therefore to seek riches that shall perish and to put one's hope in them. It is vanity also to aspire to honours and to raise oneself to high estate. It is vanity to follow the lust of the flesh and to desire that for which later there must be grievous punishment. It is vanity to hope for long life, and to take little thought for a good life. It is vanity to attend only to the present life, and not look forward to the things to come. It is vanity to love that which passes with all speed away, and not to be hastening thither where endless joy abides.

5. Think often of that wise word: 'The eye is not satisfied with seeing, nor the ear filled with hearing.' Be zealous therefore to separate your heart from the love of things which are seen, and to turn it to the things which are not seen, for those who follow their carnal nature defile their conscience, and lose the grace of God.

TWO

On Personal Humility

1. Every man naturally wants to know, but what is the good of knowledge without the fear of God? Indeed, a humble peasant who serves God, is better than a proud philosopher, who ponders the course of the sky, but neglects himself. He who knows himself well becomes cheap in his own eyes, and takes no pleasure in the praises of men. If I should know everything in the world, but should be without love, what would it avail me in God's presence, he who will judge me by my deeds?

2. Rest from too great a desire to know, because therein is found great discord and delusion. Learned men are very eager to appear, and to be called learned. There is much which it profits the soul little or nothing to know. And foolish indeed is he who gives his attention to other things than those which make for his salvation. Many words do not satisfy the soul, but a good life refreshes the mind and a pure conscience offers great confidence towards God.

3. The greater and better your knowledge, so much the more severely will you be judged, unless you have lived a more holy life. Do not therefore be lifted up for any skill or learning, but rather fear for the knowledge that has been given you. If it seems to you that you know much and understand well enough, know also that there is much more which you do not know. 'Do not be high-minded', but rather confess your ignorance. Why do you wish to set yourself ahead of another, when more may be found with greater learning than you and more skilled in law? If you wish to know, and to learn anything to good purpose, be eager to be unknown and accounted nothing.

4. This is the highest knowledge and the most useful lesson – to have true understanding and small opinion of oneself. To hold no high opinion of oneself, and always to judge well and highly of others, is great wisdom and high perfection. If you should see another openly do wrong, or commit some grievous sins, you should not reckon yourself better than he, because you do not know how long you may be able to continue in integrity. We are all frail, but you must not count anyone more frail than yourself.

On Teaching the Truth

1. He is a happy man whom truth itself instructs, not by semblances or transient voices, but precisely as it is. Our thoughts and our feelings often deceive us, and perceive but little. What profit is there in great argument about hidden matters and obscure, ignorance of which brings us no condemnation in judgment? It is great unwisdom if, setting aside the useful and the necessary, we give attention without cause to things frivolous and damaging. Having eyes, we see not.

2. What do 'kinds' and 'species' matter to us? He to whom the eternal Word speaks is freed from many opinions. From the one Word are all things, all things proclaim one Word; and this is the Beginning, which also speaks to us. Without it no man understands or rightly judges. He to whom all things are one, and who relates all things to one, and sees all things in one, can be steadfast in heart and abide at peace in God. O God, the Truth, make me one with you in never-ending love. I am often wearied in reading and hearing many things. In you is all I wish for and desire. Let all who teach fall silent, let all things created remain speechless before you. Do you alone speak to me.

3. The more a man is made one with himself, and simple in heart, the more and deeper matters and without effort he comprehends, because he receives the light of understanding from above. A pure, simple, steadfast spirit is not torn apart amid a multitude of tasks, because he does all things for the honour of God, and strives within himself to be at rest from all self-seeking. What hinders and burdens you more than your heart's unmortified condition? A good and devoted man first orders in his own heart the tasks which fall to him among men. They do not draw him to desire what a faulty, bent nature does, he brings them to the decision of sound reason. Who has a harder battle than he who strives to conquer himself? And this must be our endeavour, in a word, to subdue ourselves, day by day to gain the mastery of self and make progress towards something better.

4. All perfection in this life has some imperfection attached to it, and none of our observation is without some darkness. A humble understanding of yourself is a surer path to God than deep inquiry into knowledge. Not that knowledge is to be held at fault, nor any simple understanding of what is considered good in itself and set in place by God, but a good conscience and a virtuous life is ever to be preferred. But because more people strive rather for knowledge than good lives, for that reason they often stray, and bear almost no fruit or little. O, if men would only summon up as much diligence in rooting out vices and planting virtues, as they do in raising questions, there would not arise such evils in society, nor such laxity in the cloister! For sure, when the day of judgment comes, inquiry will not be made of us what we have read, but what we have done, not how well we have spoken, but how piously we have lived. Tell me – where now are all those teachers and masters whom you knew well while they yet lived, and were eminent in learning? Already others hold their positions, and I know not whether they think back on them. In their lives they seemed to be something, but now there is no word of them.

5. O, how swiftly passes the glory of the world! Would that their life had been in agreement with that which they knew.

Then would they have studied and read well. How many perish through empty learning in this world and care little for the service of God. And because they choose rather to be great than humble they fade away amid their own speculations. He is truly great who has great love. He is truly great who is small in his own eyes and holds as nothing every peak of honour. He is truly wise who holds all earthly things as trash, that he may make Christ his gain. And he is truly learned who does the will of God, and abandons his own will.

FOUR

On Prudence in Action

1. Not every word and impulse is to be trusted. A matter must be cautiously and patiently weighed before God. Alas! Often evil is believed and spoken more readily about another than good. So weak we are. But mature people do not easily believe every teller of tales, because they know that human weakness is prone to evil and unreliable enough in speech.

2. It is great wisdom not to rush into action nor obstinately to hold our own opinions. It is part also of this wisdom not to believe every word of man, nor to pour out promptly into others' ears what we hear and believe. Take counsel with a man of wisdom and good conscience. And seek rather to be instructed by a better person than to follow your own devices. A good life makes a man wise in the sight of God, and gives him experience in many things. As each is in himself humbler and more subject to God, the wiser will he be in all things and the more at peace.

On Reading the Holy Scriptures

1. Truth is to be sought in the Holy Scriptures, not skill in words. Every sacred scripture should be read in the spirit in which it was written. We must seek rather usefulness in the Scriptures than subtlety of speech. That is why we must be as ready to read devotional and simple books, as those which are deep and profound. And let not the authority of the writer stumble you, whether he be of small or of great skill in letters, but let the love of truth draw you on to read. Do not ask who said this but take heed to what is said.

2. Men pass away, but the truth of the Lord endures for ever. Without respect of persons, God speaks to us in many ways. Our curiosity often hinders us in the reading of the Scriptures, when we want to understand and to discuss, when we should pass simply on. If you wish to absorb well, read with humility, simplicity and faith. Never wish to have a name for knowledge. Ask freely for the words of holy men and listen silently. Let not the hard sayings of men older than yourself displease you. They are not put forward without cause.

On Controlling Desire

1. Whenever a man longs for anything beyond measure immediately he is disturbed within. The proud and the covetous are never at rest. The poor and the humble in spirit live in the fulness of peace. The man who is not yet truly dead to self is quickly tempted and defeated in small and trifling things. The one who is weak in spirit, and in some manner still carnal, and prone to the things of sense, finds it difficult to withdraw completely from earthly longings. And for that reason he is often sad when he does withdraw himself. He is also easily angered if anyone opposes him.

2. But if he pursues his inclination, he is immediately burdened by the accusation of his conscience, because he has followed his passion which avails him nothing in his search for peace. Therefore true peace of heart is found in resisting passions, not by yielding to them. There is therefore no peace in the heart of the carnal man, nor in a man devoted to the things around him, but only in the fervent and the spiritual.

SEVEN

On Avoiding Empty Hope and Elation

1. Vain is he who puts his hope in men or in anything created. Let it not shame you to serve others for the love of Jesus Christ and to be counted poor in this world. Do not depend upon yourself, but establish your hope in God. Do what is in your power, and God will be with your good will. Trust not in your own knowledge, nor in the cleverness of anyone alive, but rather in the grace of God who helps the humble, and brings low those who presume upon themselves.

2. Boast not in riches if you have them, nor in friends because they are powerful, but in God who provides all things, and above all things longs to give himself. Do not exalt yourself because of the stature or beauty of your body, which, with a little sickness, can be marred and disfigured. Do not be pleased with yourself because of ability or wits, lest you displease God

from whom is the whole of every good thing you naturally possess.

3. Do not reckon yourself better than others, lest, before God, who knows what is in man, you be reckoned worse. Do not be boastful of good works, because God's judgments are other than those of men, and what pleases men often displeases him. If you have anything good, reckon others to have better things, that you may preserve humility. It does no harm to place yourself below all others, but it does the utmost harm to put yourself above even one other. Perpetual peace is with the humble, but in the heart of the proud there is envy and frequent wrath.

EIGHT

On Avoiding Too Great Familiarity

1. Do not reveal your heart to every man, but discuss your case with one who is wise and fears God. Be seldom with young people and strangers.

2. Do not fawn upon the rich nor be eager to appear in the presence of the great. Seek the company of the humble and simple, with the devout and gentle, and let your conversation be about that which builds you up. Do not be familiar with any woman, but commend all good women equally to God. Pray to be familiar with God alone and his angels, and avoid the notice of men.

3. Show love to all men, but familiarity is not profitable. It sometimes happens that someone, though unknown, shines from a good reputation, whose presence, however, is displeasing to the eyes of those who look at him. We sometimes think to please others by our company, and straightway displease them from the faultiness of character observed in us.

On Obedience and Submission

1. It is truly a great thing to live in obedience, to be under authority and not independent. A state of subjection is far safer than a position of authority. Many are in a state of obedience more from necessity than love, and they take it amiss, and repine for no great cause. And they do not regain liberty of mind unless they submit themselves wholeheartedly for God's sake. Run here or there: you will not find rest save in humble submission to the rule of one set over you. Thinking about change of abode has deceived many.

2. It is true that everyone likes to do as he desires and is disposed rather to those who agree with him. But if God is among us it is necessary sometimes to give up our own opinion for the boon of peace. Who is so wise that he fully knows everything? Do not therefore put too great a trust in what you think, but rather listen willingly to others' opinions. Though what you think is good, and for God's sake you put this aside, and follow another, you will profit the more by it.

3. I have heard often that it is safer to accept counsel than to give it. It can even happen that each one's opinion is good, but to be unwilling to listen to others, when reason or occasion demands, betokens pride and wilfulness.

TEN

On Avoiding Too Many Words

1. Avoid as far as you can the noisy presence of men, for involvement in the affairs of the world is a great hindrance, though they come our way with innocent intent. For we are quickly soiled and snared by vanity. I could wish often that I had remained silent, and not been in the company of men. But why do we so readily talk and chat together, when we return to silence so rarely without damage to our conscience? We talk so readily because we seek mutual consolation, and hope to ease our heart grown weary with much thinking. And we are very pleased to speak and think of the things we love much and desire, or else those things we most dislike.

2. But alas! It is often to no purpose and in vain, for this outward consolation is often no small hindrance to the consolation God can give within. Therefore we must watch and pray that time pass not without profit. If it be permitted and appropriate to speak, speak of that which upbuilds. Bad habit and neglect of our progress much promotes unguardedness of speech. However, no small help to spiritual progress is devout conversation on spiritual things, especially where those of one mind and spirit find their fellowship in God.

ELEVEN

On Winning Peace and Eagerness for Progress

1. We might have much peace, if we were of a mind not to concern ourselves with what others say and do, and which is none of our business. How can he long remain at peace who involves himself with others' concerns, who seeks opportunities outside his sphere, and who rarely draws his inner self together? Blessed are the single-hearted for they shall have much peace.

2. Why were some of the saints so mature and thoughtful? Because it was their whole desire to die to all the things of earth, and so they were able to hold fast to God with all their inner being, and to be free for themselves. We are too much taken up with our own passions and too anxious over transitory things. Rarely do we completely overcome even a single fault, and are not zealous over our daily progress. That is why we remain cold and lukewarm.

3. If we were completely dead to ourselves and completely unbound in spirit, then we might be able to savour the things of God and experience something of heavenly contemplation. Our whole and very great hindrance is that, because we are not free from passions and from lusts, we do not try to follow the perfect pathway of the saints. When even a small trouble comes our way we are too soon cast down, and turn to earthly consolation.

4. If we would strive like strong men to stand in battle, then we should see God's help from heaven upon us. For he who himself provides occasion for battle that we might be conquerors, is ready to help those who strive, hoping in his grace. If we place our progress in religion only in those outward observances, our religious life will quickly reach its end. But let us lay the axe to the root, so that, purged of passions we may possess a mind at peace.

5. If every year we rooted out one fault, we should quickly become mature men. But, on the contrary, we often feel that we appeared better and holier at the beginning of our Christian life, than after many years of its profession. Our fervour and progress should grow day by day, but now it is taken for a great thing if one is able to retain a part of one's first ardour. If we would do ourselves a little violence at the beginning, then afterwards we should be able to act with light-heartedness and joy.

6. It is hard to surrender those things to which we have become accustomed, but it is harder to go against our own will. But if you do not overcome small and inconsiderable things, when will you conquer the more difficult? Resist your inclination at the start, and unlearn an evil habit, lest it chance to lead you little by little into greater difficulty. O, if you were to consider what great peace you would make for yourself, and what gladness for others, by controlling yourself, I think you would be more anxious for spiritual progress!

TWELVE

On the Usefulness of Adversity

1. It is good for us that at times we have sorrows and adversities, because they often make a man realise in heart that he is an exile, and puts not his hope in any worldly thing. It is good that we at times endure opposition, and that we are evilly and untruly judged, when our actions and intentions are good. Often such experiences promote humility, and protect us from vainglory. For then we seek God's witness in the heart when we are accounted cheap abroad by men, and evil is believed of us.

2. Therefore must a man so strengthen himself in God that it is not necessary for him to seek much human consolation. When a man of good will is troubled, or tested, or afflicted with evil thoughts, then he understands that he needs God more, for without him he can lay hold of nothing good. Then also he is sad, and groans and prays over the miseries he suffers. Then he is wearied of living on, and prays to reach death, that he may be dissolved and be with Christ. Then too he understands that perfect freedom from care and full peace cannot exist in the world.

THIRTEEN

On Defeating Temptations

1. So long as we live in the world we cannot be without tribulation and temptation. That is why it is written in Job: 'Man's life on earth is warfare.' And therefore everyone must be concerned about his temptations and watchful in prayer, lest the devil find opportunity for deception; for he never sleeps but 'goes about seeking whom he may devour'. No one is so mature and holy that he does not sometimes have temptations, nor can we be completely free from them.

2. Nevertheless temptations are often very useful to a man, hard and heavy though they may be, because in them a man is made humble, cleansed and instructed. All the saints passed through many tribulations and temptations and made progress. And those who were unable to bear temptations were rejected and fell away. There is no order so sacred, no place so set apart, that there are no temptations and adversities there.

3. There is no man completely free from temptations as long as he lives, because the source of temptation is in ourselves.

In that we were born in sinful desire, one temptation or tribulation passes and another is on its way, and we shall always have something to suffer, for we have lost the boon of our original felicity. Many seek to escape temptations and more grievously fall into them. We cannot win by flight alone; but by patience and true humility we are made stronger than all our foes.

4. He who merely turns aside outwardly, and does not tear out the root, will make small progress. No, indeed, temptations will return to him more quickly, and he will feel the worse. Little by little, and through patience and endurance of spirit (with God helping) you will win a better victory than by hardness of your own determination. Seek counsel more often in temptation, and do not deal hardly with one who is tempted, but pour in comfort as you might wish done to you.

5. The beginning of all evil temptations is instability of mind and small trust in God. Because, just as a ship without a helm is tossed this way and that by the waves, so a careless man who abandons his resolution, is tempted in various ways. Fire tests iron, and temptation the just man. Often we do not know what we can do, but temptation reveals what we are. Nevertheless we must watch, especially in the beginnings of temptation, for then is the foe more easily overcome when he is in no manner allowed to enter the portal of the mind, but is met outside the threshold as soon as he has knocked, and there withstood. Whence someone has said:

Resist thou the beginnings; too late comes remedy
When ills through long delays have grievous grown to
  be.

For first the mere thought meets the mind, then the strong imagination, afterwards pleasure, evil action and assent. And so, little by little, the malicious foe gains total entrance, when he is not resisted at the beginning. And the longer a man is inactive in resisting, the weaker each day he grows in himself, and the enemy stronger against him.

6. Some people suffer their most grievous temptations at the beginning of their Christian life, some at the end. Some are hard put to it throughout their whole life. Some are tempted lightly enough according to the wisdom and justice of God's ordaining which weighs the standing and the worth of men, and orders all things beforehand for the salvation of his chosen ones.

7. We must not therefore despair when we are tempted, but the more fervently beg of God that he may think fit to help us in every tribulation; who, assuredly, according to the saying of Paul, 'will with the temptation make a way of escape that we may be able to bear it'. Let us therefore humble our souls beneath the hand of God in all temptation and tribulation, because he will save and lift up those who are of a humble spirit.

8. In temptations and tribulations a man's progress is proved, and there his greater worth emerges and his virtue is more apparent. It is not a great thing if a man is devoted and ardent when he feels no affliction, but if in a time of adversity he bears himself patiently, there is hope of great progress. Some are kept safe in great temptations, and often overcome in the small ones of every day, that, brought low, they may never trust themselves in great things, who in such small things are proved weak.

On Avoiding Rash Judgment

1. Turn your eyes upon yourself and beware of judging what others do. In judging others a man toils in vain, often goes astray, and easily sins; but in judging and examining himself he often toils fruitfully. According as something is near to our heart, so frequently we judge of it; for we easily lose true judgment because of personal affection. If God were always the sole object of our desiring, we should not so easily be disturbed by opposition to our opinion.

2. But often something lies hidden within, or encounters us from without which equally draws us along. Many secretly look to their own ends in what they do, and are unaware of it. They even seem to continue in good peace when things are done according to their wish and sentiment, but if it happen otherwise than they desire, they are soon disturbed and made sad. On account of the variety of feelings and opinions, often enough dissensions arise between friends and citizens, and between godly and pious men.

3. Old habit is given up with difficulty, and no one is easily led beyond what he himself can see. If you rely more on your own reason and diligence than upon the subduing worth of Jesus Christ, rarely, and that slowly, will you become an enlightened man, because God wills that we should be completely subject to him and rise above all reason by the love that burns in us.

On Works Done out of Love

1. Evil is not to be done for anything in the world, nor for the love of any man; yet, for the benefit of one in need, a good work is at times to be openly interrupted, or even changed for something better. For if this be done, a good work is not destroyed but changed into a better. Without love an outward work profits nothing, but whatever is done from love, however so small and inconsiderable it may be, becomes completely fruitful – if indeed God's reckoning is based upon the goodwill and love with which a man acts rather than on how much he does.

2. He does much who loves much. He does much who does something well. He does well who serves the common good rather than his own will. Often that seems love which is rather carnality, for natural inclination, self-will, hope of repayment, desire for advantage, are common ingredients.

3. He who has true and perfect love seeks self in nothing, but longs only for God's glory to be manifest in everything. He envies no man for he loves no selfish joy, nor does he wish to rejoice in himself, but desires above all good things to be blessed in God. He ascribes good to no one but to God alone completely, from whom, like a fountain, all things come forth, and in whom, at the end, all the saints rest in joy. O, he who had but a spark of true love, would feel that all earthly things will prove full of vanity.

On Tolerating Others' Faults

1. Those things which a man is not strong enough to put right in himself or in others, he should endure patiently until God ordains otherwise. Consider that it is perhaps better so for your testing and your patience, without which our merits are not to be highly valued. Nevertheless you should pray about such hindrances, that God may see fit to help you, that you may be able to bear them gently.

2. If someone, though admonished once or twice, does not comply, do not strive with him, but commit it all to God, that his will may be done, and his honour shown in all his servants. He knows well how to change evil into good. Try hard to be patient in tolerating others' faults and infirmities of whatsoever kind, because you too have much which must be tolerated by others. If you cannot make yourself as you wish, how will you be able to fashion another to your liking? We are glad to see others made perfect, and yet do not correct our own faults.

3. We want others to be strictly corrected, but do not wish to be corrected ourselves. The wide licence of others displeases us, and yet we do not wish that we ourselves should be denied what we desire. We want others to be bound by rules, and yet by no means do we suffer ourselves to be more restricted. So therefore it is obvious how seldom we assess our neighbour as we assess ourselves. If all men were perfect, what then should we have to tolerate from others for God's sake?

4. But now God has so ordered it that we should each learn to bear the other's burdens, for no one is without fault, no one without a burden, no one self-sufficient, no one wise enough for himself; but it behoves us to bear with one another, console one another, equally to help, instruct and admonish. Of what worth a man is, appears best in a time of adversity, for circumstances do not make a man frail, but they do show the kind of man he is.

On the Life of a Monk

1. You must learn to break yourself in many things if you wish to maintain peace and concord with others. It is no small thing to dwell in monasteries or a religious community, and therein to live without complaint and to continue faithfully to death. He is a blessed man who has lived well there, and happily reached the end. If you wish to stand and progress as you ought, hold yourself an exile and a pilgrim on the earth. You must be counted a fool for Christ's sake if you would live a religious life.

2. The habit and tonsure count for little. It is the change of character, and complete mortification of the passions, that make a truly religious man. He who seeks anything save God entirely and the salvation of his soul, will find nothing but tribulation and sorrow. He cannot even continue long at peace, who does not strive to be the least and the servant of all.

3. You have come to serve, not to rule; know that you are called to endure and to toil, not to enjoy leisure and talk. Here, therefore, men are tried as gold in the furnace. Here no one can stand, unless with his whole heart he has determined to humble himself for God's sake.

22 *The Imitation of Christ*

On the Examples of the Holy Fathers

1. Consider the living examples of the holy fathers in whom shone real perfection and religion, and you will see how little, virtually nothing, we do. Alas, what is our life if it be compared to theirs? Saints and friends of Christ, they served the Lord in hunger and thirst, in cold and nakedness, in toil and weariness, in watchings and fastings, in prayers and holy meditations, in persecutions and many reproaches.

2. O, how many and grievous tribulations did the Apostles, Martyrs, Confessors and Virgins suffer, and the rest who desired to follow the steps of Christ! For they hated their lives in this world that they might keep them to life eternal. O, what a strict and renounced a life did the holy fathers in the desert live! What long and grievous temptations they endured! How often were they harried by the enemy! What frequent and fervent prayers did they offer up to God! What stern fastings did they practise! What mighty zeal and fervour had they for spiritual progress! What strong war they waged against the tyranny of their vices! With what pure and upright effort did they reach for God! By day they laboured, and at night they gave themselves to long-continued prayer, though while they laboured they ceased not at all from mental prayer.

3. They spent their whole time usefully, every hour seemed short to spend with God; and in the great sweetness of contemplation even the need of bodily refreshment was surrendered to forgetfulness. They renounced all riches, dignities, honours, friends and relations; they desired to have nothing from the world; they took the bare necessities of life; they were grieved to serve the body, even in necessity. Therefore they were poor in earthly things, but most rich in grace and virtues. Outwardly they were in want, but within they were refreshed with God's consolation.

4. To the world they were strangers, but to God they were neighbours and familiar friends. To themselves they seemed nothing, and to this world despised; but in the eyes of God they were precious and beloved. They stood in true humility, they lived in simple obedience, they walked in love and patience; and so day by day they advanced in spirit and obtained great favour with God. They have been given for an example to all men of religion and should call us to good progress, more than the number of the lukewarm call us to careless living.

5. O, how great was the ardour of all men of religion at the beginning of this holy institution! O, what devoutness of prayer! What rivalry of virtue! How great a discipline flourished! What reverence and obedience under the master's rule blossomed in all things! The traces left until now bear witness that they were truly holy and mature men, who, so strongly warring, trod down the world. Now a man is thought great if he is not a sinner, and if he can endure with patience the task in hand.

6. O, the lukewarmness and negligence of our estate, that we so quickly swerve from our old ardour, and it now becomes a weariness to live from sloth and lukewarmness! May progress in the virtues not wholly sleep in you, who many times have seen the examples of devoted men.

On the Discipline of a Good Man of God

1. The life of a good religious man must be mighty in virtues, that he should be inwardly what he appears outwardly to men. And rightly he should be more within than he appears without, since God is our examiner whom we should reverence supremely, wherever we may be, and, as the angels do, walk pure in his sight. Every day we should renew our resolution, and stir ourselves to fervour, as if today we had first come to conversion and to say: 'Help me, Lord God, in good resolution and in your holy service, and grant me now today to make a perfect beginning, because what I have hitherto done is nothing.'

2. According to our resolution, so is the rate of our progress, and he needs much diligence who desires much progress. And if one of strong resolve often falls short, how shall it be with him of rare or less determined resolve? Yet abandonment of resolution comes about in many ways, and a small omission in our exercises scarcely passes without some loss. The resolution of the just depends rather on the grace of God than upon their own wisdom, in whom also they ever trust whatever they lay hold of, for man proposes but God disposes, and a man's way is not in himself.

3. If for pity's sake or the purpose of a brother's benefit an accustomed exercise is at times omitted, it can easily be taken up later. But if for weariness of mind or negligence it is lightly relinquished, that is blameworthy enough, and the hurt will be felt. Strive as we may, yet still shall we fail a little in many things. Nevertheless, some certain resolution must be made, especially against those things which most hinder us. We

must examine and order both our inner and our outer life, since both contribute to our progress.

4. If you are not able continually to consider yourself, do so anyway at times, and at least twice a day, morning, namely, and evening. In the morning make your resolutions, in the evening inquire into your conduct, of what sort you were today in word, and deed, and thought, for in these things you have perhaps more often offended God and your neighbour. Gird yourself like a man against the devil's evils. Bridle gluttony, and you will more easily bridle every urge of the flesh. Never be completely unoccupied, but be reading, writing, praying, meditating or doing something useful for the common good. Bodily exercises, however, must be undertaken with discretion, nor are they to be taken up by all alike.

5. Those duties which are not common to all, are not to be shown in public, for what is private is more safely carried out in secret. Care must, however, be taken that you are not slothful in common duties, and more ready to do what is private, but when you have fully and faithfully carried out your duties and commands, if there is then further time available, give yourself to yourself, as your devotion leads you. All cannot have one exercise, but one suits this person better and another that. Even according to the appropriateness of the time different exercises are suitable, some pleasing better on festival days and some on common days; we need others in a time of temptation, and others in a time of peace and quietness. There are some we are pleased to think on when we are sad, others when we are happy in the Lord.

6. Around the time of the great festivals, good exercises should be renewed, and the intercessions of the saints more

fervently besought. From festival to festival we should make our resolutions, as if then we were about to depart from this world and came to the eternal festival. And so more earnestly we should prepare ourselves in times of devotion, and more devoutly live, and more strictly keep each observance, as if in a short time we were to receive from God the reward of our labour.

7. And if this be deferred, let us believe ourselves not well enough prepared, as yet unworthy of so great a glory, which shall be revealed in us at the appointed time; and let us be zealous to prepare ourselves better for departure. 'Blessed is the servant,' as the Evangelist Luke says, 'whom, when the Lord comes, he shall find watching. Truly, I tell you, he will set him over all that he has.'

TWENTY

On the Love of Solitude and Silence

1. Seek a proper time for yourself and think often upon the blessings of God. Leave aside mere curiosity. Read such matters as may sting your conscience, rather than merely fill your time. If you will but withdraw yourself from unnecessary conversations and idle going about, and indeed from listening to news and common talk, you will find sufficient and proper time for profitable meditations. The greatest of the saints used to avoid as much as they could the company of men, and chose to live for God in seclusion.

2. Someone has said: 'Whenever I have been among men, I have returned a lesser man.' We often experience this when we have spent a long time in conversation. For it is easier to

be completely silent, than not to exceed in speech. It is easier to lie hidden at home than to be able sufficiently to guard oneself abroad. He, therefore, who seeks to reach that which is hidden and spiritual must with Jesus slip away from the crowd. No one can safely appear in public who does not enjoy seclusion. No one safely talks but he who gladly keeps silent. No one safely rules but he who is glad to be subordinate. No one safely commands but he who has learned well to obey.

3. No one safely rejoices but he who has the testimony of a good conscience within. Even the tranquillity of the Saints was full of the fear of God. Nor were they the less earnest and humble within themselves because they shone with great virtues and grace. But the boldness of the wicked arises from pride and presumption, and turns in the end to their own deception. Never promise yourself freedom from care in this life, however good a monk or devout hermit you may be.

4. Often those who stand best in the estimation of men are the more gravely endangered because of their too great confidence. Therefore it is more profitable for many that they should not entirely be without temptations, but should be often attacked, lest they be too confident, lest they should be lifted into pride, or turn aside too easily to the consolations that are outside themselves. O, he who never seeks a passing gladness, never engages himself with the world, what a good conscience would he keep! O, he who cuts off vain anxiety, and meditates simply on helpful and godly matters, and establishes his whole hope in God, what great peace and quietness would he possess!

5. No one is worthy of heavenly consolation who has not diligently exercised himself in holy self-reproach. If you wish

to be deeply rebuked in heart, go into your cell, and shut out the turmoil of the world, as it is written: 'On your beds, reproach yourselves.' You will find in your cell what you too often miss abroad. A cell continually used grows sweet, and ill-kept spawns weariness. If in the early days of your Christian life you dwell in it and keep it well, it will be afterwards a dear friend to you and a most pleasing solace.

6. In silence and quietness the devout soul makes progress and learns the hidden things of the Scriptures. There it finds streams of tears in which each night it washes and cleanses itself, that it may be made more familiar with its creator, according as it dwells apart from all the tumult of the times. He who therefore withdraws from acquaintances and friends, to him God with his holy angels will draw near. It is better to lie hid and take care of oneself, than, neglecting oneself, work miracles. It is praiseworthy for a religious man to be seen rarely abroad, to escape from being seen, even to have no wish to see men.

7. Why do you wish to see what you cannot have? 'The world passes away and the lust thereof.' The desires of sensuality draw you to walk abroad, but when an hour has passed what do you bring back but heaviness of conscience and destruction of the heart? Often glad departure brings a sad return, and late evenings a sad morning. So does all carnal joy enter pleasantly, but in the end it gnaws and destroys. What can you see elsewhere that you cannot see here? Behold heaven and earth and all the elements, for of these are all things made.

8. What can you see anywhere, which can long remain, beneath the sun? You think perhaps to have all you want, but you will not be able to reach this. If you could see all things at once before you, what would it be but an empty vision? Lift up your eyes to God on high, and pray for your sins and omissions. Leave vain things to vain people, but do you attend to the things which God has commanded you. Shut the door upon yourself and call Jesus, your beloved, to you. Remain with him in your cell, for you will not find peace so great elsewhere. If you had not gone out, and had not listened to vain talk, you would have better continued in good peace. But from the moment when, at any time, you take delight in hearing news, thereafter you must suffer disquietude of heart.

TWENTY-ONE

On the Heart's Contrition

1. If you want to make any progress, keep yourself in the fear of God, and do not wish to be too free: but curb all your senses under discipline, and do not give yourself up to foolish mirth. Give yourself to self-reproach of heart, and you will find devotion. Self-reproach opens many good things, which dissoluteness is apt quickly to lose. It is a wonder that any man in this life can be truly glad who considers and weighs his exile and the manifold perils of his soul.

2. Through levity of heart and neglect of our shortcomings, we do not feel the griefs of our soul, and often vainly laugh, when properly we should weep. There is no true liberty nor real joy, save in the fear of God with a good conscience. Happy is the man who can cast aside every hindrance of distraction, and gather himself into the oneness of holy self-examination. Happy is the man who renounces whatever can blot or burden his conscience. Strive manfully: habit is by habit overcome. If you know how to let men alone, they will readily let you alone to do what you have to do.

3. Do not busy yourself with the affairs of other people, nor get entangled with the affairs of the great. Keep an eye on yourself first of all, and admonish yourself before all your dear friends. If you have not the favour of men, do not for that reason be saddened, but let this have weight with you, that you do not hold yourself as well and circumspectly as befits a servant of God and a devout monk to conduct himself. Often it is better and safer for a man not to have many consolations in this life, especially after the flesh. Yet we are to blame that we have not, or rarely have, God's consolations, because we seek not self-reproaching of the heart, nor completely cast aside vain and outward consolations.

4. Recognise that you are unworthy of God's consolation, but worthy rather of much tribulation. When a man is humbled perfectly in heart, then the whole world is burdensome and bitter to him. A good man will find sufficient material for sorrowing and weeping. For whether he considers himself or ponders about his neighbours, he knows that no one lives here without tribulation. And the more strictly he considers himself, so much the more he grieves. Materials for just grief and inner self-reproaching, are our sins and vices, in which we lie so enwrapped, that rarely are we able to give our thoughts to heavenly things.

5. If you would think more frequently of your death than length of life, there is no doubt that you would strive more ardently to amend yourself. If, too, you were to consider in your heart more carefully the future pains of hell or purgatory, I believe that willingly you would endure toil and grief, and

would dread no austerity. But because these things do not reach the heart, and we love the things which flatter us, so we remain cold and truly slothful.

6. Often it is through poverty of spirit that the wretched body so readily complains. Pray therefore humbly to the Lord that he may give you the spirit of self-reproach, and say with the Prophet: 'Feed me, Lord, with the bread of tears and give me to drink tears in abundance.'

TWENTY-TWO

On Pondering Man's Wretchedness

1. You are unhappy wherever you are, in whatever direction you turn, unless you turn to God. Why are you troubled that things do not turn out for you just as you wish and desire? Who is there who has everything according to his wish? Neither I, nor you, nor any man on earth. There is no one on earth free from trouble or anguish, be he king or Pope. Who is he who has a better lot? Assuredly he who has the strength to suffer something for God.

2. Many foolish weaklings say: 'Look, what a good life that man has, how rich, how great, how powerful and exalted.' But give your attention to the good things of heaven, and you will see that all those things of time are nothing, but utterly uncertain and more burdensome because they are never held without anxiety and fear. The happiness of a man is not in having temporal things in abundance, but moderation is enough for him. To live on earth is truly wretchedness. The more a man desires to be spiritual, the more bitter the present life becomes to him, because he better understands and sees more clearly the shortcomings of man's corruption. For to eat, to drink, to stay awake, to sleep, to rest, to labour, and to submit to the other necessities of nature, is truly great wretchedness and affliction to a devout man, who would gladly be released and free from all sin.

3. For the inner man is greatly burdened in this world by the demands of the body. And so the Prophet devoutly asks for strength to be free from them saying: 'From my distresses deliver me, O Lord.' But woe to them who do not recognise their wretchedness, and more to them who love this wretched and perishable life. For some so strongly cling to it (though even by toil or begging they have scarcely what they need), that, if they could always live here, they would have no care for the kingdom of God.

4. O, mad and faithless in heart, who so buried lie in earthly things, that they relish nothing but the things of the flesh! But, wretched even now, in the end they will sadly understand, how cheap and worthless was that which they loved. But the saints of God, and all devoted friends of Christ, gave no thought to the things which pleased the flesh, nor which flourished in this life, but their whole hope and aspiration panted for the good things of eternity. Their whole desire was borne upwards to the things which will abide and cannot be seen, lest by love of things visible they should be borne to the things below.

5. Do not, my brother, lose confidence in spiritual progress, you still have time and opportunity. Why do you wish to put off your progress till tomorrow? Rise, and begin this moment and say: 'Now is the time for action, now is the time to fight, now is the proper time to amend.' When you are in bad

case and troubled, then is the time to win merit. You must go through fire and water before you come to refreshment. Unless you apply force to yourself, you will not conquer vice. So long as we bear about this frail body, we cannot be without sin, nor live without weariness and sorrow. We would gladly have rest from all misery, but because through sin we have lost innocence, we have lost also true blessedness. And so we must hold to patience and await the mercy of God, until iniquity pass away, and this mortality be swallowed up in life.

6. O, how great the frailty of man, ever prone to vices! Today you confess your sins, and tomorrow you commit again the sins you have confessed. Now you resolve to be on guard, and after an hour you so act as if you never had resolved. Deservedly then we can humble ourselves, and never hold any high opinion of ourselves, because we are so frail and unstable. Swiftly, too, that can be lost through negligence, which with much toil we have scarcely won by grace.

7. What in the end will yet become of us, who so early grow lukewarm? Woe to us if we so wish to turn aside to rest, as if already there were peace and safety, when there does not yet appear in our manner of living a trace of pure holiness. There is good need that we be yet again instructed, like good novices, in the best morality, if perchance there is any hope of future amendment and greater spiritual progress.

TWENTY-THREE

On Thinking of Death

1. Very quickly it will be all over with you here; consider how it is with you in another life. Man is today, and tomorrow he

appears not. When he has been moved from sight, quickly, too, he passes from the mind. O, the dullness and hardness of the human heart, that it thinks only of what is at hand, and looks not rather forward to what shall be! In every deed and thought you should so bear yourself, as if you were forthwith about to die. If you had a good conscience you would not much fear death. It is better to watch against sin than fly to death. If today you have not prepared, how will you be tomorrow? Tomorrow is an uncertain day, and how do you know whether you will have tomorrow?

2. What profit is long life, when we make amends so little? Ah, long life does not always amend us, but often increases guilt the more. Would that for one day we could conduct ourselves well in this world. Many count up the years since they were converted, but often how little fruit of improvement there is. If it is a dreadful thing to die, perhaps it is more perilous to go on living. Happy is he who always has the hour of death before his eyes, and daily prepares himself to die. If you have ever seen a man die, consider that you will pass the same way.

3. When it is morning, think that you will not live till evening. When evening comes dare not promise yourself the morning. Be therefore always prepared, and so live that death will never find you unprepared. Many die suddenly and unexpectedly. For 'at the hour that you think not the Son of Man will come'. When that last hour comes, you will begin to think far otherwise of all your past life, and you will greatly grieve that you have been so negligent and remiss.

4. How happy and prudent is he who strives so to be in life, as he prays to be found in death! For complete contempt for the world, an ardent longing to progress in virtues, love of discipline, the toil of penitence, readiness to obey, self-abnegation, and endurance of any adversity for the love of Christ, will give great confidence of dying happily. Many are the good things you can do while you are well; but when health fails, I do not know what you will be able to do. Few are made better by ill-health; so too those who wander much abroad, rarely grow more holy.

5. Do not trust in friends and neighbours, nor put off your salvation till the future; for men will forget you more quickly than you think. It is better now to make timely provision and send some good ahead, than to trust in the help of others. If you are not anxious for yourself now, who will be anxious for you in the future? Now is time very precious. Now is the day of salvation, now is the acceptable time. But alas, the sorrow, that you do not spend this time more profitably in which it is in your power to win merit, whence you may live eternally. The time will come when you will long for one day or hour for amendment, and I know not whether you will obtain it.

6. O, dearly beloved, from what great peril you will be able to free yourself, from what great fear escape, if only you will be always fearful and looking towards death! Be zealous now so to live that in death's hour you may be able rather to rejoice than fear. Learn now to die to the world, that then you may begin to live with Christ. Learn now to hold all things of small value, that you may be able to go freely to Christ. Chastise your body now in penitence, that then you may be able to have sure confidence.

7. Ah, fool, why do you think that you will live a long time when here you have no day secure? How many are deceived and snatched unexpectedly from the body. How often have

you heard people say that one died by the sword, another was drowned, another fell from a high place and broke his neck, another collapsed while eating, another met his end at play, one by fire, another by steel, another by plague, another died by brigandage; and so the end of all is death, and the life of man like a shadow suddenly passes away.

8. Who will remember you after death? And who will pray for you? Do now, do now, dearly beloved, whatever you can do, because you do not know when you will die, you do not even know what will happen to you after death. While you have time gather for yourself wealth that does not perish. Think of nothing but your salvation; care only for the things of God. Make friends for yourself now by venerating the saints of God, and by imitating their deeds, so that when you falter in this life, 'they may receive you into everlasting habitations'.

9. Keep yourself as a pilgrim and stranger upon earth, who has no concern with the business of the world. Keep your heart free and lifted up to God because you have not here 'a continuing city'. To him direct your prayers and daily groanings with tears, that your spirit may deserve after death to pass happily to God. Amen.

TWENTY-FOUR

On Judgment and the Punishment of Sinners

1. In all things have regard to the end, and in what fashion you will stand before a strict judge, to whom nothing is hidden; who is not appeased by gifts, nor accepts excuses, but will judge what is just. O, most miserable and foolish sinner, what will you reply to God who knows all your misdeeds who sometimes dread the face of an angry man? Why do you not provide for yourself on the day of judgment, when no man will be able to be excused or defended by another, but each one will be sufficient burden to himself? Now is your toil fruitful, your weeping acceptable, your groaning heard, your grief satisfactory and cleansing.

2. The patient man, who, suffering wrongs, is more grieved over another's malice than the harm done to him, who prays gladly for his adversaries, forgiving their faults from his heart, who is not slow to ask pardon of others, who is quicker to pity than to wrath, who often does violence to himself, and strives to subject the flesh to the spirit completely, he has a great and healthy source of cleansing. It is better now to purge our sins and cut back our vices, than to keep them to be purged in the future. Truly we deceive ourselves through the inordinate love we have for the flesh.

3. What else will that fire devour but your sins? The more you now spare yourself and follow the flesh, the more you shall pay hereafter, and store up more fuel for burning. In those things in which a man has most sinned, in those he will be the more grievously punished. There the slothful will be stabbed with blazing goads, the gluttons will be tormented with enormous hunger and thirst. The wanton and the pleasure-lovers will be drenched in blazing pitch and stinking sulphur, and the envious will howl in pain like rabid dogs.

4. There will be no vice without its appropriate torment. There the proud will be filled with all confusion, and the greedy crushed with most grievous want. There, one hour in punishment will be more grievous than a hundred years in bitterest penance here. There, will be found no rest, no

consolation for the condemned. Here there is sometimes rest from labour, and enjoyment of the consolations of friends. Be now anxious and in sorrow for your sins, that in the day of judgment you may be carefree with the blest. For then the just shall stand in great steadfastness against those who have pressed upon them and held them down. Then shall he who has humbly submitted himself to the judgments of men, stand up to judge. Then shall the poor and humble have great confidence, and the proud will fear on every side.

5. Then he who has learned to be a fool and despised for Christ, will seem to have been wise in this world. Then will all tribulation patiently borne seem pleasing, and all iniquity shall stop its mouth. Then shall every devout man rejoice, and every profane man shall mourn. Then shall the afflicted flesh exult more than if it had been ever nourished with delights. Then shall mean garments shine and well-woven clothes turn dingy. Then the poor little dwelling shall be praised more than the gilded palace. Then shall steadfast patience more avail than all the power in the world. Then shall simple obedience be more exalted than all worldly cleverness.

6. Then shall a pure, good conscience delight more than learned philosophy. Then shall contempt of riches weigh more than all the treasures of the sons of earth. Then shall you find more consolation in having devoutly prayed than in having feasted sumptuously. Then shall you rather rejoice in having kept silence, than in having talked much. Then shall holy deeds be of more value than many fair words. Then shall a life of discipline and hard penance be more pleasing than any earthly delight. Learn now to suffer in small things that you may be able to be delivered in things more grievous. Try out here first what you may be able to endure hereafter. If

you are not strong enough to bear so little now, how will you be able to endure eternal torments? If a little suffering makes you so impatient now, what then shall Gehenna do? Look, truly you cannot have two joys, to delight yourself here in this world, and afterwards to reign with Christ.

7. If, up to this very day, you had ever lived in honour and in pleasures, what advantage would all of it bring to you, if now in the present moment it should befall you to die? All therefore is vanity save to love God and serve only him. For he who loves God with his whole heart, fears neither death nor punishment, nor judgment, nor hell, because perfect love gives sure access to God. But he who still finds delight in sin, no wonder is it if he fears death and judgment. Yet it is good that, if love does not yet reclaim you from evil, the fear of Gehenna should at least restrain you. For he who truly puts off the fear of God, will not long be able to persevere in good, but will quickly fall into the devil's snares.

TWENTY-FIVE

On the Ardent Amendment of the Whole Life

1. Be watchful and diligent in the service of God, and often reflect: 'Why have you come here? And why have you abandoned the world? Was it not that you might live for God and become a spiritual man?' Therefore be ardent for progress, because you will soon receive the reward for your labours, and then neither fear nor sorrow shall come within your borders any more. You will labour a little now, and you will find great rest, yea everlasting joy. And if you continue ardent and faithful in what you do, God beyond doubt will be faithful in rewarding you. You must hold fast the hope

that you will reach the crown, but you must not lay hold of security lest you grow slothful and lifted up.

2. When a certain anxious person wavered often between fear and hope, on one occasion, overwhelmed with sadness, he threw himself down in a church before an altar, saying as he turned these matters in his mind: 'O, if I only knew that I should still persevere!' – immediately he heard God's reply in his heart: 'And if you knew this, what would you want to do? Do now what you would then want to do, and you will be perfectly secure.' And immediately, consoled and comforted, he committed himself to God's will, and his anxious wavering ceased. And he had no wish for curious searching to know what would happen to him but studied rather to learn what God's well-pleasing and perfect will might be for the beginning and perfecting of every good work.

3. 'Hope in God and do good,' says the Prophet, 'and inhabit the land and feed upon its wealth.' There is one thing that keeps many back from progress and heart-felt amendment: dread of the difficulty or the toil of the struggle. Assuredly, they more than all others advance in the virtues who more manfully strive to overcome those things which are more hard and opposed to them. For there a man most profits and merits more abundant grace, where most he overcomes himself and mortifies the spirit.

4. But all people have not equally as much to overcome and mortify. Yet a zealous imitator will make more valiant progress, though he have more passions, than another who is gentle in character but less ardent for the virtues. Two things especially conduce to great amendment: to wit, forcibly to withdraw from that to which nature is viciously inclined, and to press earnestly towards the good which we each most lack. Strive, too, more to guard against and overcome those things which displease you most in others. Lay hold upon advancement everywhere, so that, if you hear or see good examples, you may be fired to imitate. But if you have thought anything blameworthy, take care lest you do the same; or, if at times you have done so, be zealous the more quickly to correct yourself. How pleasant and how sweet it is to see brethren, ardent and devout, well-mannered and disciplined! How sad and grievous to see them walk disorderly, not practising those things to which they were called! How hurtful it is to neglect the purpose of their calling and to turn the heart to that which is not their business!

5. Be mindful of the purpose of which you have laid hold, and set before you the image of the crucified. You can be truly ashamed when you look upon the life of Jesus Christ, because you have not yet been zealous the more to be like him, though you have been long in the way of God. The religious man who exercises himself intensely and devotedly in the most holy life and passion of the Lord, will find there abundantly all things useful and necessary for him. Nor is there need to seek anything better outside Jesus. O, if Jesus crucified should come into our heart, how quickly and adequately should we learn!

6. The ardent religious man receives and bears well all things which are commanded him. The negligent and lukewarm religious man has tribulation on tribulation, and suffers anguish on every side, because he lacks inner consolation, and is forbidden to seek that which is without. The religious man who lives outside of discipline, is exposed to grievous ruin. He who seeks things easier and less restrained, will

always be in troubles, because one thing or the other will always displease him.

7. How do so many other religious men do who live beneath restraint enough under cloistered discipline? They seldom go out, live apart, eat in the poorest fashion, dress roughly, labour much, speak little, keep long vigil, rise early, prolong prayer, read much, and keep themselves in all discipline. Consider the Carthusians, the Cistercians, and the monks and nuns of other religious orders: how they rise each night to sing praises to the Lord. And a base thing it would be for you to grow slothful in such holy work, when such a host of religious people are beginning to sing praise to God.

8. O, if no other obligation lay upon us than with the whole heart and voice to praise the Lord our God! O, if you should never need to eat, or drink or sleep, but could always praise God and be free for spiritual pursuits alone! Then you would be much more happy than now, when you serve the flesh and every sort of need. Would to God those needs did not exist, but only the spiritual refreshments of the soul, which, alas, we savour rarely enough.

9. When a man reaches this point, that he seeks his consolation from no created thing, then first does God begin perfectly to content him; then, too, will he be well content with every outcome of events. Then will he neither rejoice for much, nor be sorrowful for little, but commit himself wholly and trustingly to God, who is all in all to him; to whom, assuredly, nothing is lost or perishes, but all things live for him, and at his nod instantly obey.

10. Remember always the end, and that time lost does not return. Without care and diligence you will never acquire virtues. If you begin to grow lukewarm, you will begin to deteriorate. But if you give yourself to zeal, you will find great peace and will feel labour lighter, for the grace of God and the love of virtue. An ardent and diligent man is ready for everything. It is a greater toil to resist vices and passions than to sweat at bodily labours. He who does not shun small faults, gradually slips into greater. You will always rejoice in the evening, if you spend the day fruitfully. Watch over yourself, stir yourself up, admonish yourself, and whatever may be the case with others, do not neglect yourself. You will progress in proportion as you do violence to yourself.

BOOK TWO

Advice About the Inner Life

ONE

On Inner Fellowship

1. 'The Kingdom of God is within you,' says the Lord. Turn with your whole heart to God, and abandon this wretched world, and your soul will find peace. Learn to despise that which is without, and give yourself to that which is within, and you will see the kingdom of God come in you. For the kingdom of God is peace and joy in the Holy Spirit, which is not given to the godless – Christ will come to you, revealing his own consolation, if you have prepared for him a dwelling-place. All his glory and beauty is within, and there he is pleased to dwell. His visits are many to the inner man, sweet discourse, gracious consolation, great peace, and fellowship most marvellous.

2. Come now, faithful soul, prepare your heart for this bridegroom, that he may deign to come to you and dwell in you. For so he says: 'If any man loves me, he will keep my word, and we will come to him and make our abode with him.' Give, therefore, place to Christ and deny entry to all others. When you have Christ you are rich and have sufficient. He will be your provider and faithful watchman in everything, so that there is no need to hope in men. For men swiftly change and fast disappear; but Christ abides for ever, and stands firmly right to the end.

3. There is no great confidence to be placed in man, frail and subject to death, even though he be useful and dear to us; nor should we entertain much sorrow from him, if occasionally he oppose or speak against us. Those who today are with you, tomorrow can be against you, and often change to the contrary direction like the wind. Put your whole confidence in God, and let him be your fear and love. He will answer for you, and will bless as shall be better. You have here no 'continuing city', and wherever you are, you are a stranger and a pilgrim; nor will you ever have rest, unless you are firmly knit to Christ within.

4. Why do you look round you here, when this is not the place of your resting? Your home must be in heavenly places, and all things earthly are to be viewed as if you were passing by. All things pass away, and you equally with them. See that you do not become involved, lest you are snared and perish. Let your contemplation be on the Most High, and let your supplication without ceasing be directed to Christ. If you do not know how to explore high and heavenly things, rest in the passion of Christ, and dwell willingly in his sacred wounds. For if devoutly you make your flight to the wounds and precious marks of Christ, you will sense great comfort in tribulation; nor will you care much for the slights of men, and will easily bear the words of detractors.

5. Christ was despised on earth by men, and in his greatest need, amid insults, was abandoned by those who knew him and by friends; and you dare to complain of anyone? Christ had his adversaries and slanderers; and you wish to have everyone as friends and benefactors? Whence will your patience win its crown if it has encountered nothing of adversity? If you wish to suffer no opposition, how will you be Christ's friend? Endure with Christ and for Christ, if you wish to reign with Christ.

6. If once you have completely entered into the heart of Jesus, and tasted a little of his burning love, then you will care nothing for your own convenience or inconvenience, but will rejoice rather at the reproach brought on you, because the love of Jesus makes a man despise himself. One who loves Jesus and truth, a true man of the spirit, free from undisciplined affections, can freely turn to God, lift himself above himself in spirit, and fruitfully rest.

7. He who tastes all things as they are, and not as they are reputed and reckoned to be, this man is wise and instructed more by God than men. He who knows how to walk from within and give small weight to things without, does not wait for places or times, for devout exercises of devotion. The spiritual man quickly gathers himself together, because he never squanders himself wholly on external things. No outward labour, or occupation, at the moment needful, stands in his way, but as events turn out, so he adapts to them. He who is rightly organised and ordered within, is not concerned over the wondrous and perverse doings of men. A man is hindered and distracted, as he draws things to himself.

8. If it were well with you, and you were truly cleansed, all things would work together for your good and profit. That is why many things displease you and often disturb you, because you are not yet truly dead to yourself and separated from all earthly things. Nothing so soils and entangles the heart of man as an impure love for created things. If you renounce outward consolation, you will be able to contemplate heavenly things and frequently rejoice within.

TWO

On Humble Submission

1. Do not weigh highly who may be for you or against you. But take thought and care that God be with you in everything you do. Have a good conscience, and God will defend you well. For him whom God has willed to aid, no perverseness of man will be able to harm. If you can keep silence and endure, you will see without a doubt the help of God. He himself knows the time and manner of delivering you, and so you must yield yourself to him. It is God's part to help and to deliver from all confusion. It often avails much in keeping deeper humility that others know and rebuke our failings.

2. When a man humiliates himself for his failings, then he easily calms others, and without difficulty satisfies those who are angry with him. God protects and liberates the humble, loves and consoles the humble, inclines to the humble man, bestows great grace upon the humble, and when he has been cast down, he lifts him up to glory. To the humble he reveals his secrets, and sweetly draws and invites him to himself. The humble, when rebuke has been accepted, is well enough at peace, because he stands in God and not in the world. Do not reckon yourself to have progressed at all, unless you feel yourself to be inferior to all.

THREE

On the Good and Peaceful Man

1. First keep yourself in peace, then you will be able to bring peace to others. A peaceful man is more useful than a very learned man. A passionate man even turns good into evil, and easily believes evil. A good, peaceful man turns everything to good. He who is truly at peace, is suspicious of no one, but he who is discontented and restless, is stirred by various suspicions, is neither at rest himself, nor permits others to be at rest. He often says what he should not say, and leaves undone what it most behoves him to do. He has his mind on what others are bound to do, and does not do what he is bound to do. Therefore, first of all, be zealous over yourself, then justly you will be able to be zealous over your neighbour.

2. You know well how to excuse your own deeds and set them in a good light, and are not willing to accept the excuses of others. It would be more just to accuse yourself, and excuse your brother. If you wish to be borne with, do you bear with others. See how remote you are still from the true love and humility, which knows not to be angry and indignant with anyone, except only with oneself. It is no great matter to mingle with the good and gentle, for this is naturally pleasing to everybody, and every one of us prefers peace and loves more those who are likeminded. But to be able to live at peace with hard, contrary men, undisciplined and up against us, is great grace, most praiseworthy and a manly deed.

3. There are those who keep themselves in peace, and even have peace with others. And there are those who neither have peace nor let others go in peace; they are troublesome to others but always more troublesome to themselves. And there are those who keep themselves in peace and strive to bring others back to peace. Nevertheless all our peace in this wretched life is rather to be placed in humble suffering, than in not feeling adversities. He who knows better how to suffer will hold the greater peace. He is the conqueror of self and

the master of the world, the friend of Christ and the heir of heaven.

FOUR

On the Pure Mind and Singleness of Purpose

1. On two wings a man is raised above earthly things, namely, sincerity and purity. There must be sincerity in the aims we set before us, purity in affection. Sincerity reaches out for God, purity lays hold of him and tastes him. No good work will hinder you, if you are free within from undisciplined affection. If you have naught else in mind and aim but what is well-pleasing to God and useful to your neighbour, you will truly enjoy liberty within. If your heart were right, then every created thing would be a mirror of life, and a book of sacred doctrine. There is no creature so small and worthless that it does not show forth the goodness of God.

2. If you were good and pure within, then you would see everything without impediment, and would understand it well. The pure heart penetrates heaven and hell. As each one is within, so he judges outwardly. If there is joy in the world, this, assuredly, the man of pure heart possesses. And if there is anywhere tribulation and anguish, an evil conscience is the more aware of it. Just as iron put in the fire loses rust, and is made all glowing, so the man who turns wholly to God is stripped of slothfulness, and is changed into a new man.

3. When a man begins to grow lukewarm, then he fears small labour, and willingly accepts consolation from without. But when he begins completely to subdue himself, and manfully

to walk in the path of God, then he counts less those things which earlier seemed to him to be grievous.

On Knowing Oneself

1. We cannot place too little confidence in ourselves, because grace and understanding are often lacking in us. Little light is in us, and this we lose through negligence. Often we do not notice because we are so blind within. Often we act wrongly and make worse excuses. Sometimes we are moved by passion and think it zeal. We blame small things in others, and pass over greater things in ourselves. Quickly enough we feel and weigh up what we endure from others; but how much others bear from us we do not notice. He who well and rightly weighs his own shortcomings, cannot pass severe judgment on another.

2. The spiritual man who sets care of himself above all cares, and who diligently attends to himself, easily keeps silence about others. You will never be spiritual and devout, unless you keep silence about things that do not concern you, and particularly pay heed to yourself. If you direct your attention wholly to yourself and God, little will move you that you perceive abroad. Where are you when you are not present to yourself? And when you have run through all things, what progress have you made, if you have neglected yourself? If you desire to have peace and true unity, you must put aside all the rest, and have yourself only before your eyes.

3. Equally you will make much progress if you keep yourself free from all temporal care. You will greatly fail, if you set

your mind on anything temporal. Let nothing be to you great, high, pleasing, acceptable, save simply God or God's affairs. Think wholly empty, whatever consolation comes from any thing created. The soul that loves God despises anything beneath God. God alone is eternal, beyond measure, filling all things, the solace of the soul and the heart's true joy.

SIX

On the Joy of a Good Conscience

1. The glory of a good man is the testimony of a good conscience. Keep a good conscience and you will always have gladness. A good conscience can bear exceeding many things, and is exceeding glad amid adversity. A bad conscience is always afraid and uneasy. Sweetly you shall rest, if your heart does not condemn you. Never rejoice unless you have done well. The bad never have true gladness, and do not experience peace within, for 'there is no peace to the wicked', says the Lord. And if they have said: 'We are in peace, evils shall not come on us, and who will dare to harm us?', believe them not; because suddenly surges forth the wrath of God, and their deeds are brought to nothing, and their thoughts will perish.

2. To glory in tribulation is not a burden to the one who loves, for so to glory is to glory in the cross of the Lord. The glory given and received of men is short. Sadness always goes with the glory of the world. The glory of the good is in their consciences, and not in the mouth of men. The gladness of the just is from God, and in God, and their joy is from the truth. He who desires true and eternal glory, does not care for the temporal. And he who seeks temporal glory and does not wholeheartedly despise it, is shown to love heavenly glory less. He has great peace of heart who cares neither for praises nor revilings.

3. He will be easily content and brought to peace, whose conscience is clean. You are not more holy if you are praised, nor the baser if you are reviled. You are what you are; nor can be called better than what you are in God's estimation. If you give heed to what you are in yourself, you will not care what men say about you. 'Man looks upon the outward appearance but God upon the heart.' Man considers deeds, but God weighs the heart's desires. It is the mark of a humble spirit, always to do good, and to set small store by oneself. It is a sign of great purity and confidence within, not to wish for consolation from any creature.

4. Clearly, he who seeks no witness outside himself, has committed himself completely to God. For, as Saint Paul says: 'Not he who commends himself is approved, but he whom God commends.' To walk with God in spirit, and not to be held by any affection outside, is the state of a spiritual man.

SEVEN

On Loving Jesus Beyond all Else

1. Happy is he who understands what it is to love Jesus, and for Jesus' sake to despise himself. He must abandon one love for another, for Jesus wills to be loved alone above all things. The love of a created thing is deceiving and unstable. The love of Jesus is faithful and goes on for ever. He who clings to a created thing will fall with what can fall; he who embraces Jesus will be established for ever. Love him and keep him as your friend, who, when all retreat, will not abandon you,

nor suffer you to perish in the end. You must, one day, be sundered from all, whether you wish or not.

2. Keep yourself near Jesus, in life and in death, and commit yourself to his faithfulness, he who, when all fail, alone avails to save you. The one you love is such by nature that he admits no rival, but wills alone to hold your heart, and like a king to sit on his own throne. If you knew how to rid yourself of every created thing, Jesus would be glad to dwell in you. You will find all lost, whatever, outside Jesus, you commit to men. Trust not, nor lean upon, 'a reed shaken by the wind'; because 'all flesh is grass and all its glory will fall like the flower of grass.'

3. Quickly will you be deceived, if you look only at the outward appearance of men. For if you look for solace and gain in others, you will more often experience loss. If you seek Jesus in everything, assuredly you will find Jesus; but if you seek yourself, you will even find yourself, but to your own destruction. For if a man does not seek Jesus, he is much more harmful to himself, than the whole world and all his enemies.

EIGHT

On Close Friendship with Jesus

1. When Jesus is there all is good, and nothing seems difficult. When Jesus is not there everything is hard. When Jesus does not speak within, consolation is worthless, but if Jesus speaks but one word, great consolation is felt. Did not Mary Magdalene immediately rise from the place where she sat weeping when Martha said: 'The Master is here and is calling you'? Happy hour when Jesus calls you from tears to

the joy of the soul! How dry and hard you are without Jesus! How witless and vain, if you desire anything outside Jesus! Is not this greater loss than if you should lose the whole world?

2. What can the world give you without Jesus? To be without Jesus is grievous hell, and to be with Jesus sweet paradise. If Jesus is with you, no enemy will be able to harm you. He who finds Jesus finds good treasure, nay, good beyond all good. And he who loses Jesus, loses exceeding much, and more than the whole world. He is most poor who lives without Jesus, and most rich who is well with him.

3. It is a great art to know how to live with Jesus, and great wisdom to know how to hold him. Be humble and a man of peace, and Jesus will be with you. Be devout and still, and Jesus will remain with you. You can quickly send Jesus away and lose his grace, if you wish to turn aside to external things. And if you have driven him away and lost him, to whom will you fly, and whom then will you seek as friend? Without a friend you cannot live well, and if Jesus is not to be to you a friend above all, you will be truly sad and desolate. You do foolishly, therefore, if you trust or find joy in any other. To have the whole world against you is to be preferred to having Jesus offended in you. Therefore, of all things dear, be Jesus alone your special love.

4. Let all be loved for Jesus' sake, but Jesus for himself. Jesus Christ is to be loved apart from all others, he who only is found good and faithful beyond all friends. For his sake and in him, let friends, equally with foes, be dear to you. And for all these prayer must be made, that all may know and love him. Never desire to be praised or loved apart from all others, because this belongs to God alone, who has no other like himself. Nor wish that anyone, in his heart, should be taken up with you, nor that you should be taken up with the love of anyone; but let Jesus be in you and in every good man.

5. Be pure and free of heart without entanglement with any created thing. You must be stripped and carry a pure heart to God, if you wish to be unhindered, and to see how sweet the Lord is. And in truth you will not attain to this unless you be led and drawn on by his grace, that, with all else cast off and dismissed, alone you are at one with God alone. For when the grace of God comes to a man, then he is equipped for all things, and when it leaves him, then he will be poor and weak, as if abandoned to lashes alone. In these things you are not to be cast down or despair, but calm in mind stand by the will of God, and endure all things which come upon you to the praise of Jesus Christ, because after winter summer comes, after night returns the day, and great calm after storm.

NINE

On Lack of all Comfort

1. It is not hard to despise man's comfort when God's is at hand. It is a great thing, indeed truly great, to be able to be without man's comfort and God's alike, and for the love of God be willing to bear the exile of the heart, and in nothing seek oneself or look to one's own merit. What great matter is it if you are cheerful and devout when grace comes to you? That is the hour for which everybody longs. He rides pleasantly whom the grace of God carries. And what wonder if he feels no weight who is carried by the omnipotent one, and led by the highest guide of all.

2. We are glad to have something to comfort us, and it is with difficulty that a man is freed from himself. The holy martyr, Lawrence, overcame the world, and also his Priest; because he despised everything which seemed delightful in the world, and for the love of Christ, he even gently bore God's High Priest, Sixtus, whom he loved, to be taken from him. And so by the love of his maker he overcame the love of man, and, instead of human consolation, he chose rather what was well-pleasing to God. So do you, too, learn to abandon some friend near and dear to you for the love of God. Nor take it hard when you have been abandoned by a friend, because we must all at length be separated from one another.

3. A man must strive mightily and long within himself, before he learn completely to overcome himself, and draw his whole affection to God. When a man stands upon himself he slips easily towards human consolations. But the true lover of Christ, and the zealous follower of virtues, does not fall back on those comforts, nor seeks such delights as can be felt, but rather stern exercises and the bearing of hard labours for Christ.

4. When, therefore, spiritual consolation is given by God, receive it with giving of thanks, and understand that it is the gift of God, and not what you deserve. Do not be uplifted, nor rejoice too much or foolishly presume, but be more humble from the gift, more careful and more fearful in all your doings; because this hour will pass, and temptation will come. When consolation has been removed, do not at once despair, but with humility and patience await God's visitation, because God is able to give back to you greater grace and consolation. This is no new thing nor strange to those who have had experience of the way of God, because in all the Saints and in the Prophets of old, there was often such manner of change.

5. So it was that one said while God's grace was yet with him: 'I said in my prosperity, I shall never be moved.' But he went on to say when God's grace had departed: 'You turned your face from me and I became troubled.' Meanwhile, however, he never despaired, but more urgently asked God and said: 'To you, Lord, will I cry, and make my prayer to God.' At last he makes known the fruit of his supplication, and testifies that he has been heard, saying: 'The Lord heard and pitied me; the Lord has become my helper.' But in what? 'You have turned,' he said, 'my mourning into joy, and surrounded me with gladness.' If it was so done with great Saints, we, weak and poor, must not despair, if we are sometimes warm and sometimes cold, for the spirit comes and goes as is well-pleasing to its will. And so the blessed Job says: 'You come to him at dawn, and suddenly test him.'

6. In what, therefore, can I hope, or in what must I put my trust, save in the great mercy of God and in the hope of heavenly grace? For whether good men be with me, devout brethren or faithful friends, holy books and fair discourses, sweet songs and hymns, all these help little and give little satisfaction, when I am deserted by grace, and left in my own poverty. Then there is no better remedy than in patience and self-denial in the will of God.

7. I have never found anyone so religious and devout who did not on occasion experience withdrawal of grace, or sense a cooling of ardour. No saint was so enraptured or enlightened, who was not sooner or later tempted. For he is not worthy of lofty contemplation of God, who for God's

sake is not exercised by some tribulation. For temptation commonly goes before as a sign of consolation which shall follow. For heaven's consolation is promised to those proved by temptations. 'To him that overcomes,' he says, 'I will give to eat of the tree of life.'

8. But God's consolation is given that a man may be stronger to bear adversities. Temptation follows, too, that he may not be elated by the blessing. The devil does not sleep, nor is the flesh yet dead; therefore cease not to prepare yourself for battle, for there are enemies on the right hand and the left who never rest.

TEN

On Gratitude for God's Grace

1. Why do you seek rest when you are born to labour? Dispose yourself for patience more than comforts, and for carrying the cross more than for joy. Who, too, of living men, would not gladly receive consolation and spiritual joy, if he could always obtain it? For spiritual consolations excel all the delights of the world and the pleasures of the flesh. For all worldly delights are either empty or shameful; but spiritual delights alone are pleasant and honourable, spring from virtues, and are poured forth by God into pure minds. But no one can enjoy those heavenly consolations just when he so desires, because the time of temptation ceases not for long.

2. False liberty of spirit and great confidence in self, goes much against a visitation from on high. God does well in giving us the grace of consolation, but man does ill in not returning it all to God in giving thanks. And for that reason the gifts of grace cannot flow in us who are ungrateful to their author, and do not pour back the whole to the spring from which it came. For grace is always owed to him who worthily returns thanks, and what is commonly given to the humble, is taken away from the proud.

3. I desire no consolation which takes from me the sting of conscience; nor do I aspire to consolation which leads to pride. For all that is high is not holy, nor every sweet thing good, nor every longing pure, nor everything that is dear pleasing to God. Gladly I accept grace by which I am found more humble and fearful, and am made more ready to abandon self. One taught by the gift of grace, and made wise by the blow of its withdrawal, will not dare to attribute any good thing to himself, but rather will confess himself poor and naked. Give to God what belongs to God, and ascribe to yourself what is yours; that is: render to God gratitude for grace, but to yourself alone consider owing fault, and punishment to fit the fault.

4. Put yourself always in the lowest place, and the highest shall be given you, for the highest cannot be without the lowest. The highest saints of God are the least in their own eyes, and the more glorious they are, the more humble in themselves. Full of truth and heavenly glory, they are not desirous of vain-glory. Founded and established in God, they are in no wise able to be proud. And those who ascribe to God the whole of any good they have received, 'seek not glory from one another but desire the glory that is of God alone', and wish that God in himself and in all his saints be praised above all things, and strive always for that very end.

5. Be grateful, therefore, for the smallest thing and you will be worthy of receiving greater. Let the least be in your eyes even as the greatest, and the most inconsiderable as a special

gift. If the worth of the giver be in mind, no gift will seem small or too cheap, for that is not small which is given from God most high. Even if he has given chastisements and blows, we must be grateful, because he always acts for our salvation, whatever he allows to happen to us. Let him who would hold fast the grace of God be grateful for grace given, and patient when it is taken away. Let him pray that it returns; let him be wary and humble lest he lose it.

ELEVEN

On the Fewness of Those who Love the Cross of Christ

1. Jesus has now many who love his heavenly kingdom, but few who carry his cross. He has many who desire consolation, but few who desire tribulation. He finds more to share his table, few his fasting. All wish to rejoice with him, few want to bear anything for him. Many follow Jesus to the breaking of bread, but few to drinking the cup of suffering. Many revere his miracles, few follow the shame of his cross. Many love Jesus so long as adversity does not befall them. Many praise and bless him, so long as they receive some consolations from him. But if Jesus should hide himself and leave them for a little while, they fall into complaining or deep dejection.

2. But those who love Jesus for Jesus' sake, and not for any consolation of their own, bless him in all tribulation and anguish of heart, just as in the highest consolation. And if it is his will never to give consolation, they would nevertheless always praise him, and always wish to be grateful.

3. O, what power has the pure love of Jesus, unmixed with any selfish gain or love! Should they not be all called mercenary

who are always seeking consolations? Are they not rather proved lovers of themselves than of Christ, who are always thinking of their own advantages and gain? Where shall be found one who is willing to serve God for nothing?

4. Rarely is to be found one so spiritual that he is stripped of everything. For who shall find one truly poor in spirit and detached from every created thing? 'His value is from afar, indeed from the uttermost shores.' If a man has given all his possessions, it is still nothing; and if he has done great penance, it is still a small thing; and if he has grasped all knowledge, he is still far off; and if he has great virtue, and most warm devotion, still much is lacking to him – one thing undoubtedly which is most needful to him. And what is that? That having given up all things, he give up himself, and go utterly out of himself and retain nothing of his self-love. And when he has done all that he knows should be done, that he should feel he has done nothing.

5. Let him not give great weight to what might appear so to be, but pronounce himself in truth an unprofitable servant, just as the Truth says: 'When you have done all that has been bidden you, say: We are unprofitable servants.' Then truly you will be able to be poor and naked in spirit, and with the Prophet say: 'I am poor and needy.' Yet no one is richer than he, no one more potent, no one more free, who knows how to abandon self and reckon himself the lowliest.

TWELVE

On the Royal Way of the Holy Cross

1. This saying seems hard to many: 'Deny yourself, take up your cross and follow Jesus.' But much harder it will be to hear

that final word: 'Depart from me, accursed ones, into eternal fire.' For those who gladly hear now the word of the cross and follow, shall have nothing then to fear from the hearing of eternal condemnation. This sign of the cross shall be in the heaven, when the Lord shall come to judgment. Then all the servants of the cross who have conformed in life to the Crucified, shall come to Christ the Judge with great confidence.

2. Why therefore do you fear to take up the cross, through which is the road to the kingdom? In the cross is salvation, in the cross life, in the cross protection from our foes; in the cross is the inflow of heaven's sweetness, in the cross strength of mind, in the cross joy of the spirit; in the cross is the height of virtue, in the cross perfection of holiness. There is no salvation for the soul, nor hope of eternal life, save in the cross. Take up, therefore, your cross and follow Jesus, and you will go into eternal life. He went ahead of you bearing his own cross, and died for you upon the cross, that you, too, might bear your cross, and aspire to die upon the cross. For if you should have died with him, equally, too, you shall live with him; and if you have been a partner of his suffering, you will be a partner of his glory too.

3. Look, it all consists in the cross, and it all lies in dying; and there is no other way to life and true peace within, save the way of the holy cross, and daily counting ourselves dead. Go where you wish, seek whatever you shall wish, and you will not find a higher way above, nor a safer way below, save the way of the holy cross. Dispose and order all things according to your own wish and observation, and you will only find that, willingly or unwillingly, you must suffer something, and so you will ever find the cross. For either you will feel pain of body, or you will endure tribulation of the soul within.

4. Sometimes you will be abandoned by God, sometimes you will be stirred up by your neighbour, and, what is more, often you will be a burden to your very self. Yet you will not be able to find release or alleviation in any remedy, but must endure while God so wills. For God wills that without consolation you should learn to suffer tribulation, and that you should utterly subject yourself to him, and from tribulation become more humble. No one so feels Christ's suffering from the heart, like the one to whom it has befallen to suffer in the same way. The cross, therefore, is always ready and everywhere is waiting for you. You cannot escape wherever you run, because wherever you come you carry yourself with you, and always you will find yourself. Turn above, turn below, turn without, turn within; and in all these places you will find the cross, and everywhere you must maintain patience, if you wish to have peace within and merit the eternal crown.

5. If you willingly carry the cross, it will carry you and lead you to your desired haven, where assuredly will be the end of suffering, although that will not be here. If you carry it unwillingly, you make a burden for yourself, and load yourself the more, and yet you must uphold it. If you cast away one cross, undoubtedly you will find another, and perhaps a heavier one.

6. Do you think to escape what no mortal has been able to pass by? Who of the Saints in the world was without a cross and tribulation? For Jesus Christ, our Lord, was not one hour without the anguish of his suffering. 'It behoved Christ to suffer,' he said, 'and to rise from the dead, and enter into his glory.' And how do you seek another way than this royal way, which is the way of the holy cross?

7. The whole life of Christ was a cross and martyrdom; and do you seek for yourself quietness and joy? You are wrong, you are wrong, if you seek other than to suffer tribulations, because the whole life of man is full of miseries, and set about with crosses. And the higher one has progressed in spirit, so the heavier he will often find the crosses, because the pain of his exile grows from love.

8. But yet this man so variously afflicted is not without the relief of consolation, because he feels great fruit is multiplying for him from the suffering of his cross. For while willingly he submits to it, every burden of tribulation is turned into confidence of divine consolation. And as the flesh is wasted more through affliction, so much the more is the spirit strengthened through grace within. And sometimes he is so comforted by aspiration for tribulation and adversity, through love of oneness with the cross of Christ, that he would not wish to be without sorrow and tribulation, because he believes that he is so much the more acceptable to God, as he has been able to bear more and heavier burdens for him. That is not the virtue of man, but the grace of Christ, which so prevails and acts in frail flesh, that, in fervour of spirit, it draws near to and loves what naturally it always loathes and flees.

9. It is not in the nature of man to bear the cross, to love the cross, to buffet the body and bring it into servitude, to bear insults willingly, to despise oneself and desire to be despised; to bear any adversities and losses, and to long for no prosperity in this world. If you look to yourself, you will not be able of yourself to do any of this; but if you trust in the Lord, strength will be given you from heaven, and the world and the flesh shall be subjected to your sway. But you shall not even fear your enemy, the devil, if you have been armed by faith and marked by the cross of Christ.

10. Set yourself therefore, like a good and faithful servant of Christ, to the manful carrying of the cross of your Lord, crucified because of love for you. Prepare yourself to bear many adversities and various trials in this wretched life, because so it shall be with you wherever you shall be, and so in truth you will find it wherever you shall hide. So it must be, and there is no means of escaping evil's tribulation and sorrow, save by bearing them. Drink in love the Lord's cup, if you desire to be his friend, and have part in him. Leave consolations to God; with such things let him do as most pleases him. But do you set yourself to the bearing of tribulations, and consider them the greatest consolations for 'the sufferings of this time are not worthy to be compared with the future glory to be won, which shall be revealed in us' – even if you were able to endure them all alone.

11. When you reach this point that tribulation is sweet and savoursome to you for Christ, then consider it is well with you, because you have found paradise on earth. So long as suffering is a burden to you and you seek to escape, so long it will be ill with you, and tribulation will follow you everywhere.

12. If you set yourself to what you should, namely, to suffer and to die, you will soon be made better, and will find peace. Though you had been snatched to the third heaven with Paul, you are not for that reason secure from suffering evil. 'I will show you,' says Jesus, 'what you must suffer for my name.' Therefore, it remains to you to suffer, if it is your wish to love Jesus and serve him for ever.

13. Would that you were worthy to suffer something for Jesus' name; what great glory would await you, what exaltation for all the saints of God, what encouragement also for your neighbour! For everyone commends patience, though few are willing to suffer. Surely, you should suffer a little for Christ, when many suffer more heavily for the world.

14. Know for certain that you must live your life while dying. And as each one dies the more to self, so the more he begins to live for God. No man is fit for the understanding of heavenly things unless he has submitted himself to bearing adversities for Christ. Nothing is more acceptable to God, nothing more healthy for you in this world, than suffering willingly for Christ. And if you had to choose you should rather pray to suffer adversity for Christ, than to be refreshed by many consolations, because you would be more like Christ, and more in conformity with all the saints. For our merit, and the advancement of your state, consists not in many delights and consolations, but in bearing great troubles and tribulations.

15. If, indeed, there had been anything better and more useful to man's salvation than to suffer, Christ would assuredly have shown it by word and deed. For both the disciples who follow him, and all those desiring to follow him, he clearly exhorts to carry the cross, saying: 'If anyone wishes to come after me, let him deny himself, and take up his cross and follow me.' With all things, therefore, read and examined, let this be the last conclusion: 'Through many tribulations we must enter the kingdom of God.'

BOOK THREE

On Consolation Within

On Christ's Secret Speech with the Faithful Soul

1. 'I will hearken to what the Lord God says within me.' Blessed the soul which hears the Lord speaking within, and receives the word of consolation from his lips. Blessed are the ears which pick up the rills of God's whisper, and pay no attention to the whisperings of this world. Blessed are the ears which listen, not to the voice which sounds abroad, but the one which teaches truth within. Blessed are the eyes closed to things without, but fixed on those within. Blessed are they who go deep within, and work hard to prepare themselves more and more by daily exercises to receive the secrets of heaven. Blessed are they who are eager to have leisure for God, and shake themselves free from every hindrance of the world. Give your attention to this my soul, and close the doors of your carnal nature, that you may be able to hear what the Lord your God says within you.

2. These things says your beloved: 'I am your salvation, your peace and your life. Keep by me and you will find peace.' Dismiss all passing things and seek those which are eternal. What are all temporal things, but seductions? And what avail all things created if you will be deserted by the Creator? Therefore, with all else put away, give back yourself, acceptable and faithful, to your Creator, that you may be able to grasp true blessedness.

On How Truth Speaks Within Without the Din of Words

1. 'Speak, Lord, because your servant hears. I am your servant. Give me understanding that I may know your testimonies. Incline my heart to the words of your mouth. Let your speech flow as the dew.' Once the children of Israel would say to Moses: 'Do you speak to us, and we will hear. Let not the Lord speak to us lest perchance we die.' Not so, Lord, not so, do I pray, but rather, with Samuel the Prophet, humbly and longingly I make supplication: 'Speak, Lord, because your servant hears.' Let not Moses speak to me, or any of the Prophets, but do you rather speak, Lord God, who inspired and enlightened all the Prophets; because you alone, without them, can perfectly instruct me, but they, without you, will profit nothing.

2. They can, indeed, sound words, but cannot convey the spirit. They speak most beautifully, but, with you silent, they do not fire the heart. They hand scriptures on to us, but you open up the meaning of the signs. They issue commands, but you help to perform them. They show the way, but you give strength to walk in it. They function only outside of us, but you instruct and enlighten the heart. They water the surface, but you give fertility. They cry aloud with words, but you give understanding to the hearer.

3. Let not Moses, therefore, speak to me, but you, O Lord, my God, Eternal Truth, lest I die and prove fruitless, if I shall have been admonished without, but not fired within; and lest the word heard, but not done, known, but not loved, believed, and not kept, serve for judgment against me. 'Speak, therefore,

Lord, because your servant hears; for you have the words of eternal life.' Speak to me, for some sort of comfort to my soul, and for the mending of my whole life, but to your praise and glory and everlasting honour.

On How God's Words are to be Heard Humbly

1. 'Hear, my son, my words, my words most sweet, going beyond all the learning of the philosophers and wise men of this world. My words are spirit and life, and are not to be weighed by human understanding. They are not to be subjected to empty approbation, but heard, in silence, and to be taken up with all humility and great love.'

2. And I said: 'Blessed is the man whom you have instructed, Lord, and taught him concerning your law, that you may give him rest from evil days, and he be not desolate upon the earth.'

3. 'I,' said the Lord, 'taught the Prophets from the beginning, and up till now cease not to speak to all; but many are deaf to my voice and hard. Many hear more willingly the world than God; they follow more readily the appetite of their flesh than that which is well-pleasing to God. The world promises the trifles of time, and is served with great eagerness: I promise the high things of eternity, and the hearts of men are sluggish. Who serves and obeys me with such care in all things, as the world and its masters are served?' 'Blush for shame, Sidon, says the sea, and if you ask the reason, hear why.' A long journey is hurried over for small reward; for eternal life, a foot is scarce lifted from the ground by many. A cheap prize is sought; for one coin, at times, there is base strife at law; for

On Consolation Within 77

an empty matter, and small promise, men do not fear to toil day and night.

4. But, alas, the shame! for good unchangeable, inestimable reward, for the highest honour and glory without end, they are reluctant to toil even a little. Blush, therefore, slothful and complaining servant, that those are found more ready for perdition, than you for life. They rejoice more in vanity, than you in truth. Assuredly, they are not infrequently disappointed, but my promise fails no one, nor sends empty away one who trusts in me. What I have promised, I will give; what I have said, I will fulfil, if only a man remain faithful in my love to the end. I am the rewarder of all good men, and the strong examiner of all devout men.

5. Write my words upon your heart, and consider them diligently; for they will be most needful to you in time of temptation. What you do not understand when you read, you will know on the day when need arises. I come to my chosen ones in two ways, namely in temptation and consolation. And two lessons I daily read to them: one chiding their faults and the other exhorting them to increase of virtues. He who has my words and scorns them, has one who judges him on the last day.

A Prayer to Implore the Grace of Devotion

6. Lord, my God, you are all my good. And who am I that I should dare to speak to you? I am your poorest slaveling, a worm cast aside, more poor and contemptible than I know and dare to say. Remember, none the less, Lord, that I am nothing, have nothing, and am worth nothing. You alone are good, just and holy; you can do all things, are over all things, fill all things, leaving only the sinner empty. Remember your mercies and fill my heart with your grace, because you do not wish your works to be void.

7. How can I endure myself in this wretched life, unless your mercy and your grace have comforted me? Do not turn your face from me; do not delay your coming to me; do not take away your consolation, lest my soul be like earth without water in your sight. Lord, teach me to do your will. Teach me to live before you, worthily and humbly; because you who know me in truth, and knew me before the world was made, and before I was born into the world, are my wisdom.

FOUR

On the Truth and Humility with which we should have Fellowship with God

1. 'Son, walk before me in truth, and seek me always in the simplicity of your heart. He who walks before me in truth shall be guarded from evil onslaughts, and the truth shall make him free from seducers, and the slanders of the wicked. If the truth shall make you free, you shall be free indeed, and will not care for the empty words of men.' Lord, it is true, as you say; so, I beg, let it be with me. Let your truth teach me, let it guard me, and keep me safe to salvation's end. Let it make me free from every evil affection, and inordinate passion; and I shall walk with you in great liberty of heart.

2. 'I shall teach you,' says the Truth, 'what things are right and pleasing in my sight. Think over your sins with great displeasure and grief, and never think yourself to be anything because of good works. In very truth you are a sinner, exposed

to many passions and entangled by them. Of yourself you ever move towards nothing; you will quickly slip, quickly be overcome, quickly be disturbed, quickly undone. You have nothing whence you can boast yourself, but many reasons why you should count yourself worthless; because you are much feebler than you are able to understand.'

3. 'Let nothing, therefore, of all you do seem great to you. There is nothing grand, nothing precious and admirable, nothing appears worthy of repute, nothing lofty, nothing truly praiseworthy or to be desired, save what is eternal. Above all things let eternal truth please you: and let your own vast worthlessness displease you always. Fear, denounce and fly from nothing so much as your vices and your sins, which should displease you more than any loss of goods at all. Some walk before me insincerely, but, led by a certain curiosity and pride, they wish to know my secrets, and understand the deep things of God, neglecting themselves and their own salvation. These often fall into great temptations and sins, because of their pride and curiosity, for I am against them.'

4. 'Fear the judgments of God, dread the wrath of the Almighty. Do not debate the works of the Most High, but search thoroughly your iniquities, in what great matters you have fallen short, and how much good you have neglected. Some carry their devotion only in books, some in pictures, but some in outward signs and forms. Some have me on the lips, but little in the heart. There are others, enlightened in intellect and purged in feelings, who always pant after eternal things, unwillingly hear of earthly things, with sorrow obey nature's necessities; and these experience what the spirit of truth says within them, because it teaches them to despise

earthly things and love the heavenly, to neglect the world, and, day and night, long for heaven.'

On the Wondrous Effect of God's Love

1. I bless you, heavenly Father, Father of my Lord, Jesus Christ, that you have deigned to remember me in my poverty. O, Father of mercies and God of all consolation, I thank you that at times you refresh me with your consolation, unworthy of all consolation though I am. I bless you always and glorify you, along with your only-begotten Son, and the Holy Spirit, the Comforter, for ever and ever. Ah, Lord God, my holy lover, when you shall come into my heart, my whole inner being will leap with joy. You are my glory, and the rapture of my heart. You are my hope and my refuge in the day of my tribulation.

2. But because I am still weak in love and imperfect in virtue, therefore I need to be strengthened and consoled by you. Wherefore, visit me more often, and instruct in your teachings. Free me from evil passions, and heal my heart from all inordinate affections, that, made healthy within and truly cleansed, I may be rendered fit to love, strong to endure, and firm to persevere.

3. A great thing is love, a great good altogether, which alone makes light all that is burdensome, and evens out every inequality. For it bears the burden without being burdened, and makes everything bitter sweet and tasty. The noble love of Jesus drives us to the doing of great deeds, and stirs to the unending longing for greater perfection. Love wishes to rise, and not to be held back by anything beneath. Love wishes to

On Consolation Within 81

be free and apart from every worldly affection, lest its inner vision be hindered; lest for any temporal advantage it incur entanglements, or be overwhelmed by adversity. Nothing is more sweet than love, nothing stronger, nothing deeper, nothing wider, nothing more pleasant, nothing fuller nor better in heaven or on earth, because love is born of God, and cannot find rest save in God above all created things.

4. The one who loves flies, runs and is glad; he is free and not bound. He gives all for all, and has all in all, because he rests in one who is supreme above all things, from whom every good thing flows and goes forth. It looks not to gifts, but turns to the giver, above all good things. Love often knows no measure, but grows warm beyond all measure. Love feels no burden, takes no thought of labours; it strives for more than it can do; it makes no plea about impossibility, because it thinks all things are open and possible to it. It is strong, therefore, for everything, and completes and brings to accomplishment many things, in which the one who does not love, fails and falls.

5. Love watches, and while sleeping does not sleep, wearied, is not tired, hemmed in, is not confined, fearful, is not disturbed, but like a living flame and burning torch, it bursts upwards and securely passes through all. If anyone loves, he knows what this voice cries. A great city in the ears of God is the burning love of the soul which says: 'You are wholly mine and I am wholly yours.'

6. Widen me in love that I may learn to savour with the inner mouth of the heart, how sweet it is to love, and in love be melted and to swim. Let me be possessed by love, rising above myself by my strong fervour and ecstasy. Let me sing a song

of love, let me follow my beloved on high, let my soul faint in your praise, exalting in love. Let me love you more than myself, and myself only because of you, and all men in you who truly love you, as the law of love, shining from you, bids.

7. Love is swift, sincere, pious, pleasant and beautiful, strong, patient, faithful, prudent, longsuffering, manly, and never seeks itself. For when anyone seeks himself, there he falls from love. Love is guarded, humble, upright, not soft, nor light, nor reaching for empty things, sober, chaste, steadfast, quiet, and self-controlled in all the senses. Love is subject and obedient to all in authority, base and despised in its own eyes, devoted to God and thankful, trusting and hoping always in him, even when God is not a sweet savour to him, because without sorrow there is no living in love.

8. He who is not prepared to suffer all things, and to stand by the will of the beloved, is not worthy to be called a lover. The lover must willingly embrace all things hard and bitter for the beloved's sake, and not to be turned away from him by any adverse circumstances.

SIX

On the Proof of a True Lover

1. 'Son, you are not yet a strong and prudent lover.' 'How so, Lord?' 'Because on account of a little opposition, you fall away from what you have begun, and too greedily seek consolation. A strong lover stands in temptations, and does not believe the skilful persuasions of the enemy. As in prosperity I please him, so in adversity I do not displease him.'

2. 'The prudent lover does not so much consider the lover's gift, as the love of the giver. He looks rather at the love than the value, and sets all that which is given below the beloved. The noble lover does not rest in the gift, but in me above every gift. For that reason all is not lost, if at times you think less well of me or of my Saints than you might wish. That good and sweet affection of which you are sometimes conscious, is the effect of present grace, and a kind of foretaste of the heavenly fatherland, about which there must be no great striving, because it goes and comes. But to fight against the evil movements of the mind which befall, and to scorn the suggestion of the devil, is a mark of virtue and great merit.'

3. 'Let not, therefore, strange fantasies disturb you, from whatever source they are thrust out. Bravely hold your purpose and upright intention towards God. It is not illusion, that sometimes you are suddenly snatched into rapture, and immediately return to the accustomed trifles of your heart. For rather you suffer them against your will, than occasion them; and so long as they displease you, and you fight against them, it is merit and not loss.'

4. 'Know that your old enemy strives altogether to hinder your desire for good, and to distract you from every holy exercise, in a word, from the contemplation of the Saints, from the devout memory of my passion, from the salutary remembrance of sins, from guarding your own heart, and from the firm purpose of growing in virtue. He plies you with many evil thoughts, that he may work weariness and terror in you, and call you back from prayer and holy reading. He hates humble confession, and, if he could, would make you cease from communion. Do not believe him, nor take thought of him, though he often stretch for you the nooses of deception.

Put it to his account when he plies you with evil and unclean things. Say to him: "Away, unclean spirit, blush for shame, miserable one, most unclean are you who bring such matters to my ears. Depart from me, worst deceiver, you shall have no part in me; but Jesus will be with me like a strong warrior, and you will stand confused. I would rather die and submit to any pain, than consent to you. Be silent and be dumb, I will not hear you further, though you contrive more troubles for me." "The Lord is my light and my salvation, whom shall I fear. Though a host should camp against me, my heart shall not fear. The Lord is my helper and my redeemer."'

5. 'Fight like a good soldier: and if sometimes you collapse for weakness, pick up greater strength than before, trusting in my more abundant grace, and take much prior heed of empty confidence and pride. On this account many are led into error, and sometimes almost slip into blindness beyond healing. Let this ruin of the proud who foolishly rely too much upon themselves, serve to warn you and keep you ever humble.'

SEVEN

On Concealing Grace Under the Control of Humility

1. 'My son, it is more salutary and safe for you to hide the grace of devotion, nor to exalt yourself, nor to speak much about it, nor to give much weight to it, but rather to despise yourself, and fear that it has been given to one unworthy of it. This feeling should not be too strongly clasped, for it can quickly be changed into its opposite. Reflect, in a state of grace, how wretched and helpless you are wont to be without it. Nor does progress in the spiritual life consist in this alone, when you have the grace of consolation, but when humble, and in self-abnegation and patience, you endure its withdrawal; so as not then to grow dull in zeal for prayer, nor to suffer all your other customary good works to fall away, but to do them willingly, as in you lies, as though with greater strength and understanding; nor completely neglect yourself, from the dryness and anguish of mind which you feel.'

2. 'For there are many, when things have not gone well with them, who became impatient or slothful. For a man's way is not always in his control, but it is God's part to give and to control, when he wills, as much as he wills, and to whom he wills, as it shall please him and no more. Many, presumptuous because of the grace of devotion, have destroyed themselves, because they have wished to do more than they were able, not considering the measure of their own littleness, but rather following the heart's impulse than the judgment of reason. And because they have presumed beyond God's pleasure, they have quickly lost grace. They have been made poor and abandoned as worthless, who had built a nest in heaven for themselves, so that, made humble and impoverished, they should learn not to fly on their own wings, but hope beneath my feathers. Those who are new and inexperienced in the Lord's way, unless they rule themselves by the counsel of the wise, can easily be deceived and mocked.'

3. 'But if they wish to follow rather what they feel than trust others with experience, the result will be dangerous to them if they refuse to be drawn back from their own conceits. Rarely, those who are wise in their own eyes suffer humbly to be ruled by others. It is better to be a little wise with humility and small understanding, than to have great stores of varied knowledge along with self-esteem. It is better for you to have little rather than much of that which can make you proud. He does not act with sufficient discretion, who gives himself

over to gladness, forgetting his former helplessness and pure fear of the Lord, which fears to lose the proffered grace. Nor does he show a very sturdy wisdom who, in adversity, or any sort of trouble, bears himself too despairingly, and thinks and feels less confidently of me than he should.'

4. 'He who wishes to be too secure in time of peace, often is found in time of war to be too cast down and full of fear. If you knew how to stay always humble and restrained within, and indeed to guide and rule your own spirit well, you would not fall so quickly into danger and indisposition. It is good advice, when the spirit of fervour has been conceived, to think deeply on what it will be like when the light is gone. When this happens, consider that the light can come back again, for I have withdrawn it for a time for a warning to you, and for my own glory.'

5. 'Often such testing is more useful than if you should have prosperity always according to your will. For work is not to be reckoned by this, that one should have more visions and consolations, or if one be skilled in the Scriptures, or placed in higher rank, than if one be grounded in true humility, and, filled with God's love, always, with purity and integrity, seeks the honour of God, thinks nothing of himself but in truth despises himself, and even rejoices more to be despised and humiliated by others than to be honoured.'

EIGHT

On Lowliness in the Eyes of God

1. Shall I speak to my Lord, who am but dust and ashes? If I shall count myself more, look, you stand against me, and my

iniquities utter true testimony, and I cannot speak against it. But if I shall abase myself, and bring myself to nothing, and divest myself of all self-esteem, and make myself the dust I am, your grace will be favourable to me, and your light near to my heart, and all esteem, however very small it be, will be drowned in the valley of my nothingness, and will perish for ever. There you show me to myself, what I am, what I was, and whither I have come 'because I am nothing and did not know it'. If I am left to myself, look, I am nothing and total weakness; but if suddenly you look upon me, immediately I am made strong and replenished with new joy. And it is right wondrous that I am suddenly lifted up and so lovingly embraced by you, I who by my own weight am being borne continually to the depths.

2. This is what your love does, freely going before me and aiding me in so many needs, guarding me too from grave dangers, and snatching me, truth to tell, from evils innumerable. For, indeed, by loving myself amiss, I lost myself, and by seeking you alone, and purely loving you, I found equally myself and you, and by love I have more deeply reduced myself to nothingness. Because, you, sweetest one, deal with me beyond all merit, and beyond what I dare to hope or ask.

3. Blessed be you, my God, because though I am unworthy of any good, your excellence and boundless kindness never cease to do good to the ungrateful, and to those who are turned far away from you. Turn us to yourself that we may be thankful, because you are our salvation, our courage and our strength.

On How Everything Must Return to God as its Final End

1. 'My son, I must be your highest and final end, if you truly wish to be happy. Out of this purpose your affection will be purified, too often wrongly bent back upon itself and upon created things. For if in anything you seek yourself, you forthwith fail within yourself, and grow dry. Therefore, first of all, refer all to me, because I am the one who has given all. So look upon each several blessing as flowing from the supreme good, and so it is that all things must be returned to me, as to their source.'

2. 'From me small and great, poor and rich, as from a living fountain, drink living water, and those who, of their own will freely serve me, will receive grace for grace. But he who will glory in anything outside of me, or take delight in any private good, will not be established in true joy, nor enlarged in his heart, but in very many ways will be hindered and hemmed in. You must, therefore, ascribe no good to yourself, nor to any man attribute virtue, but give the whole to God without whom man has nothing. I gave all, I wish to repossess all, and with great strictness I require acts of thanksgiving.'

3. 'This is truth, by which the emptiness of boasting is put to flight, and if heavenly grace and true love have entered in, there will be no envy or narrowing of the heart, nor shall self-love lay hold of you. For heaven's love conquers all things, and widens all the powers of the soul, because there is no one good save God alone, who is to be praised above all things and in all things blessed.'

On the Joy of God's Service, the World Forsworn

1. Now once more shall I speak, Lord, and not be silent; I shall say in the ears of my God and my King, who is in heaven: 'How great is the abundance of your sweetness, Lord, which you have laid up for those that fear you.' But what is there for those who love you, what for those who serve you with the whole heart? Truly unutterable is the sweetness of the contemplation of you, which you bestow on those who love you. In this you most revealed to me the sweetness of your love, that when I was not, you made me, and when I wandered far from you, you brought me back, that I might serve you, and you bade me love you.

2. O, fount of never-ending love, what shall I say about you? How shall I be able to forget you, who deigned to remember me, even after I pined away and perished? Beyond all hope you showed mercy to your servant, and beyond all merit revealed grace and friendship. What shall I return to you for this your grace? For it is not given to everyone, all things abandoned, to renounce the world and take up the monastic life. Is it a great thing that I should serve you, whom everything created is bound to serve? It should not seem a great thing for me to serve you, but this rather appears great and wondrous to me, that you deign to receive as a servant one so poor and unworthy, and to include him with your beloved ones.

3. Look, all things which I have, and with which I serve you, are yours. Yet, none the less, the other way around, you rather serve me than I you. Look, heaven and earth, which you made to serve man are at hand to you, and do each day whatever you have bidden. And this is a small thing: why you have even created and set up Angels to serve man! But it goes beyond all this that you yourself have deigned to serve man, and have promised to give yourself to him.

4. What shall I give you for all your thousand benefits? Would that I could serve you all the days of my life! Would I were able for even one day to show worthy service! Truly, you are worthy of all service, all honour and praise eternal. Truly, you are my Lord, and I your poor servant, who with all my strength am bound to serve you, and never must I grow weary in your praises. Such is my desire, such my longing; and whatever is lacking in me do you deign to supply.

5. It is a great honour, great glory to serve you, and, for your sake, to hold all things in contempt. For they shall have great grace, who, of their own will, shall subject themselves to your most holy service. They will find the sweetest consolation of the Holy Spirit, who, for love of you, have cast every carnal joy aside. They shall attain great liberty of mind, who, for your name's sake, enter on the narrow way, and have put aside all worldly care.

6. O, pleasing and delightful service of God, by which a man is truly made free and holy! O, holy state of religious servitude, which makes a man equal to the Angels, pleasing to God, a terror to demons, and praiseworthy to all the faithful. O, servitude to be embraced and ever prayed for, by which the highest good is won, and joy gained which shall abide for evermore.

ELEVEN

On How the Heart's Longing Must be Measured and Controlled

1. 'My son, you must learn yet many things, which you have not yet learned well.' 'What are they, Lord?' 'That you set your desire altogether according to my good pleasure, and be not a lover of your own self but an eager zealot for my will. Desires often fire you, and strongly drive you on; but consider whether you are more moved for my honour than your own interest. If I am in the matter, you will be well content with what I shall ordain, but if any self-seeking lies hid in it, look, this is what hinders and burdens you.'

2. 'Take care, therefore, that you do not strive too much over a preconceived idea, without taking counsel of me, lest perchance you afterwards repent, or what pleased you, and which you were eager for as something better, please you no more. For not every inclination which seems good is to be immediately followed, nor every opposite inclination straightway avoided. It is advisable at times to use restraint, even in good pursuits and wishes, lest through over-eagerness you run into discord of the mind, and make a stumbling-block for others through indiscipline, or even be suddenly disturbed and cast down by the opposition of others.'

3. 'Sometimes, indeed, you must use violence, and manfully go against an urge of the senses, and take no notice of what the flesh wants or does not want, but busy yourself more that it may be subject to the spirit, even against its will; and so long it must be buffeted and compelled to submit to servitude, until it is prepared for everything, and learns to be content with little, and to be delighted with simple things, nor murmur against any inconvenience.'

TWELVE

On the Building of Patience and Strife Against Desires

1. 'Lord God, as I see it, patience is most necessary for me; for much in this life falls out adversely. For however much I have contrived for my peace, my life cannot be without strife and grief.'

2. 'So it is, son. For I do not wish you to seek such a peace as is without temptations or does not feel adversities, but that only then you should count yourself to have discovered peace, when you have been exercised by manifold tribulations, and tried in many adversities. If you shall say you are not able to bear much, how then will you endure the fire of purgatory? Of two evils, the less is always to be chosen. In order, therefore, that you may be able to escape eternal torments yet to be, you should strive to bear for God present evils with an even mind. Do you think that the men of this world suffer nothing, or little? You will not find this to be so, even though you seek out the most voluptuous.'

3. 'But they have,' you say, 'many delights, and they follow their own pleasures, and for that reason they count their tribulations small.'

4. 'Even so, grant that they have what they wish; but how long, do you think, will it last? Look, just like smoke, those with abundance in this world will pass, and there will be no remembrance of their past joys. But even while they are still alive, they do not rest without inner bitterness and weariness

and fear. For from the very thing whence they imagine comes their delight, they often receive the punishment of sorrow. Justly it happens to them that, because beyond measure they seek and pursue pleasures, it is not without confusion and bitterness that they enjoy them. O, how brief, how false, how disordered and vile they all are! Yet, indeed, because of their drunkenness and blindness they do not understand, but like dumb beasts, for the small delight of this mortal life, they incur death of the soul. You, therefore, my son, do not go after their lusts, but turn from your desire. Delight in the Lord, and he will give you the wishes of your heart.'

5. 'For indeed, if you truly wish to know delight, and to be abundantly consoled by me, look, your blessing will be in the contempt of all worldly things and the breaking off of all lower delights, and richest consolation will, in return, be given you. And in proportion as you will withdraw yourself from all solace of created things, so in me you will find consolations more sweet and potent. But at first you will not attain these without some sorrow and toil of conflict. Longstanding habit will resist, but will be vanquished by a better habit. The flesh will murmur often but will be restrained by true fervour of the spirit. The old serpent will stir you up and provoke you, but will be put to flight by prayer; above all, by useful labour, too, great access will be blocked for him.'

THIRTEEN

On the Obedience of the Humble Subject After Christ's Example

1. 'Son, he who strives to withdraw himself from obedience, withdraws himself from grace; and he who seeks things for

himself, loses those which are common to all. He who does not willingly and freely subject himself to one above him, shows that his flesh does not yet perfectly obey him, but keeps on fighting back and protesting. Learn, therefore, quickly to submit yourself to one above you, if you choose to bring your own flesh into subjection. For the enemy without is more quickly conquered, if the inner man has not been laid waste. There is no more troublesome or worse enemy to your soul than you are to yourself, if you are not in harmony with the spirit. You must altogether assume a true contempt of yourself, if you wish to prevail against flesh and blood. Because, as yet, you love yourself beyond due measure, therefore you shrink from giving yourself over to the will of others.'

2. 'But what great thing is it, if you, who are dust and nothingness, for God's sake submit to man, when I, omnipotent and most high, who have created everything out of nothing, subjected myself humbly to man, for your sake? I became the most humble and lowly of all men, that you, by my humility, might vanquish your pride. Learn to obey, dust. Learn to humble yourself, earth and mud, and bend beneath the feet of all. Learn to break your will in all its movements and to give yourself to all subjection.'

3. 'Be hot against yourself, nor suffer the swelling thing to live in you, but show yourself so subject and utterly small, that all can walk over you and tread on you like the mud of the streets. What have you, worthless man, to complain about? What, vile sinner, can you say in answer to those who upbraid you, who have so often offended God, and many a time deserved hell? But my eye has spared you, because your soul was precious in my sight, that you might know my love and live always thankful for my benefits, and might

continually give yourself to true subjection and humility, and
patiently bear self-contempt.'

On Considering God's Secret Judgments, if we are Made Proud by Prosperity

1. You thunder forth your judgments over me, Lord, and
shake all my bones with fear and trembling, and my soul is
sore afraid. I stand amazed and consider that 'the heavens are
not clean in your sight'. If 'in angels you have found depravity',
yet spared them not, what will happen about me? The stars
have fallen from heaven, and what do I, who am dust, take
upon myself? They whose works seemed praiseworthy, have
fallen to the depths, and those who ate the bread of Angels, I
have seen delighted with the husks of swine.

2. There is no holiness, Lord, if you withdraw your hand. No
wisdom avails, if you cease to govern. No strength helps, if
you no longer preserve. No chastity is safe, unless you protect
it. No self-protection profits, if your holy watchfulness is
not there. For abandoned we sink and perish, but with you
beside us we rise up and live. Indeed, we are unstable, but
we are made firm by you; we grow chill, but are set on fire
by you.

3. O, how humbly and abjectly must I think about myself!
How must it be as nothing reckoned, if I seem to have aught
good! How profoundly must I submit myself, Lord, beneath
your unfathomable judgments, where I find myself to be
nothing other than nothing – nothing! O, mighty weight,
O, ocean which cannot be crossed, where I find nothing of

myself, save nothing altogether! Where is therefore glory's hiding place, where confidence of virtue begotten? All vainglorying is swallowed up in the depth of your judgments upon me.

4. What is all flesh in your sight? 'How shall the clay boast against him who shaped it?' How can he be lifted up in vain speech, whose heart in truth is subjected to God? The whole world shall not lift him up, whom truth has subdued. Nor shall he be moved by the mouth of all that praise him, who has established his hope in God. For even those who speak, look, they are all nothing; for they shall pass away with the sound of their words, 'but the truth of the Lord abides for ever'.

On the Obligation to Stand and Speak in Every Desirable Thing

1. 'Son, always speak like this: "Lord, if it shall so please you, let this come to pass. Lord, if it shall be for your honour, let it be done in your name. Lord, if you see that this is for my good, and approve it as useful, then grant me this to use for your honour. But take such a wish from me if you have judged it to be hurtful to me, and not profitable for the salvation of my soul." For every desire is not of the Holy Spirit, though it appear right and good to a man. It is difficult to judge truly whether a good spirit or an evil spirit drives you to want this or that, or even whether you are moved by your own spirit. Many have been deceived, at the end, who first seemed moved on by a good spirit.'

2. 'You must, therefore, desire and seek, with the fear of God and with the heart's humility, whatever occurs to the mind as a thing to be desired: and most of all, with self-resignation the whole must be committed to me, and you must say: "Lord, you know what way is better; let this or that be done as you shall will. Give what you will, as much as you will, and when you will. Do with me as you know should be done, and as is more pleasing to you, and let your honour be greater. Put me where you will, and deal freely with me in all things. I am in your hand, turn me this way or that in my course. See, I am your slave, ready for everything, because I do not wish to live for myself, but for you. Would it were worthily and perfectly!" '

A Prayer for Doing What is Well-pleasing to God

3. Grant me your grace, most merciful Jesus, that it may be with me, and work with me, and continue with me right to the end. Grant me always to desire and wish what is more acceptable to you, and the more pleases you. Let your will be mine, and let my will always follow yours, and best accord with it. Let my willing and not willing be according to your will, and let me be unable to will and not to will in any other way than you will or will not.

4. Grant me to die to all things in the world, and for your sake to love, to be despised, and to be unknown in this world. Grant me, above all desires, to rest in you, and let my heart be in peace with you. You are the heart's true peace, you its only rest; apart from you all things are hard and restless. In this peace, that is, in you alone, the one highest and eternal good, I shall sleep and take my rest.   Amen.

SIXTEEN

On the Need to Seek True Comfort in God Alone

1. Whatever I am able to desire or think for my comfort, I look for it not here but hereafter, because if I alone had all the comforts of the world, and were able to enjoy all its delights, it is certain that they could not last long. So you will not, my soul, be able to be completely comforted, nor to be wholly refreshed, except in God, the comforter of the poor, and the upholder of the humble. Wait a little while, my soul, await God's promise, and you will have abundance of all that is good in heaven. If too much out of measure you strive for that which is here and now, you will lose what is eternal and heavenly. Use the things of time, long for the things of eternity. You cannot be satisfied with any temporal goods, because you were not created to enjoy them.

2. Though you should have all good things created, you would not be able to be happy and blessed, save in God, who created all things, and continues to be all your blessedness and happiness, not of the sort which seems good and praiseworthy to the foolish lovers of the world, but such as Christ's good and faithful ones await, and which the spiritual and pure in heart, 'whose citizenship is in heaven', sometimes taste beforehand. All human solace is empty and shortlived. That is blessed and true solace, which is felt within by truth. The devout man carries with him everywhere his consolation – Jesus, and says to him: 'Be present with me everywhere, Lord Jesus, in every place, at every time.' Let this be my consolation, to be willing readily to do without all human comfort. And if your consolation be wanting, let your will and just approval be my highest consolation. For 'you will not be angry for ever, nor for all time threaten'.

SEVENTEEN

On Putting our Whole Trust in God

1. 'Son, let me deal with you as I will. I know what is good for you. You think as a man; you feel in many things as human feeling persuades you.'

2. 'Lord, it is true what you say. Your care is greater for me than any care I can take for myself. For he stands too much on chance who does not cast all his care on you. Lord, so long as my will remains straight and firm in you, do with me whatsoever shall please you. For it cannot be other than good, whatever you do about me. If you wish me to be in darkness, blessed be you, and if you wish me to be in the light, again blessed be you. If you design to console me, blessed be you, and if you wish me to suffer tribulation, be equally and ever blessed.'

3. 'Son, so must you be disposed, if you think to walk with me. So must you be ready to endure, and likewise to rejoice. So must you as willingly be poor and needy, as full and rich.'

4. 'Lord, I will suffer willingly for you, whatever you shall will to come upon me. I am willing, without difference, to take from your hand good and ill, sweet and bitter, glad and sad, and to give thanks for all things happening to me. Guard me from all sin, and I shall not fear death nor hell. Provided you do not cast me away for ever, nor blot me from the book of life, whatever of tribulation comes, it will not harm me.'

On Bearing all this World's Sorrows with Even Mind Like Christ

1. 'Son, I came down from heaven for your salvation. I took up your sufferings, not because I had to, but because love drew me, that you might learn patience, and not unworthily bear the sufferings of life. For, from the hour of my birth to my death upon the cross, I never ceased to bear sorrow, and had great lack of temporal things. I often heard many reproaches against me. I gently bore contradictions and harsh words; for benefits I received ingratitude, blasphemies for miracles, and for teaching censures.'

2. 'Lord, because you were patient in your life, chiefly in thus fulfilling your Father's command, it is well that I, poor wretched sinner, should bear myself patiently according to your will, and carry, while it is your will, for my salvation, the burden of mortal life. For though the present life seems burdensome, it is, however, made now most full of merit, through your grace, and by your example and the footsteps of your Saints, more bearable and brighter to the weak; but it is also much fuller of consolation than it had been of old under the ancient Law, when heaven's gate stayed shut; and the way to heaven seemed more hard to find, when so few cared to seek the kingdom of the heavens. But not even those who then were just and worthy of salvation, could enter the heavenly kingdom before your passion, and the ransom of your holy death.

3. O, what great thanks am I bound to render you, because you deigned to show me and all the faithful, the straight and good way to your eternal kingdom! For your way is our way; and through your holy patience we walk to you, who are our crown. If you had not gone before and taught us, who would care to follow? Alas, how far back would they remain, had they not in view your shining examples! Look, we are still lukewarm, although we have heard of your many miracles and teachings; what then would happen, had we not so great a light by which to follow you?

On Enduring Injuries and How the Truly Patient is Tested

1. 'What is it you are saying, son? Cease to complain, considering my suffering, and that of my Saints beside. "Not yet have you resisted to blood." It is a small thing you suffer compared with those who have suffered so much, so strongly tempted, so heavily tormented, in so many ways proved and tried. You should, therefore, bring back to mind the heavier sufferings of others, that you may be able to bear more easily your own slight ones. And if they do not seem slight to you, see that it is not your impatience which is doing this. Yet, whether they be small or great, be zealous to bear everything patiently.'

2. 'The better you dispose yourself to endure, so do you act more wisely and deserve more merit; you will also endure more easily, if you are diligently prepared for this, by mind and habit. Do not say: "I cannot endure this from such a man, nor are things of this kind to be borne by me, for he does me great damage, and taunts me with things I had never thought; but from someone else I will readily suffer, and such things as

I shall see should be suffered." Such thinking is foolish, for it does not take thought of the virtue of patience, nor of him by whom that virtue is to be crowned, but merely weighs people and harms done to oneself.'

3. 'He is not truly patient, who is not willing to suffer except so far as seems fit to him, and from whom he chooses. But the truly patient man takes no thought from what man, whether from his Superior, or from some equal or inferior, whether it be from a good and holy man, or from a perverse man and unworthy, that his trial comes, but without difference from any creature, howsoever much and howsoever many times adversity has befallen him, he accepts the whole gratefully from the hand of God and counts it immense gain, for nothing with God, howsoever small, yet for God's sake endured, will be able to pass without reward.'

4. 'Be, therefore, stripped for battle, if you wish to have victory. Without victory you cannot come to the crown of patience. If you are not willing to suffer, you refuse to be crowned. But if you desire to be crowned, strive manfully, endure patiently. Without toil, there is no progress towards rest, and no reaching victory without a fight.'

5. 'Make possible for me, Lord, what by nature seems to me impossible. You know that I am able to endure little, and that I am quickly cast down if the slightest adversity arises. Let any trial of tribulation be made to me, for your name's sake, pleasing and desirable; for to suffer and to be harassed for you, is most healthy for my soul.'

TWENTY

On the Confession of our own Weakness
and the Trials of This Life

1. 'I will confess my sin before you'; I will confess to you, Lord, my weakness. Often it is a small thing which casts me down and saddens me. I resolve to act bravely, but when a small temptation comes, I am in difficulty. Very inconsiderable is sometimes that from which a great temptation comes forth. And when I think myself just a little safe, when I am unaware, I find myself sometimes almost vanquished by the slightest blast.

2. Observe, therefore, Lord, my humility and frailty on all sides known to you. Be merciful and 'snatch me from the mire, that I sink not', lest I remain on all sides cast down. This is what often beats me back and confounds me in your presence, that I am so prone to falling and weak in resisting passions. Although it is not altogether with my consent, their onslaught, all the same, is still troublesome and grievous to me, and it wearies me much to live thus in daily strife. From this is my weakness made known to me, that loathsome fancies rush in much more easily than they depart.

3. Almighty God of Israel, champion of faithful souls, would that you would look upon your servant's toil and sorrow and stand by him in all things towards which he has striven. Toughen me with heaven's strength, lest the 'old man', the wretched flesh, not yet fully subdued by the spirit, prevail to dominate – against which it will be necessary to fight so long as breath remains, in this most miserable life. Alas, what manner of life is this, where tribulations and miseries are

not wanting, where everything is full of snares and foes! For as one tribulation and temptation recedes, another takes its place; but also, with the first conflict still continuing, many others arrive, unexpectedly too.

4. How can man's life be loved, with its vast bitterness and subject to so many catastrophes and miseries? How can it even be called life, when it begets so many deaths and plagues? And yet it is loved, and many seek delight in it. The world is often reproached because it is deceitful and empty; and yet it is not easily given up, because the lusts of the flesh too strongly govern it. Some things draw us to love, others to despising. 'The lust of the flesh, the lust of the eyes and the proud glory of life' draw us to love the world; but the penalties and miseries which justly follow them, bring forth hatred of the world and weariness.

5. But (alas, the sorrow of it!) a base delight overcomes the mind dedicated to the world, and it thinks there are pleasures under the nettles, because it does not see and has not tasted the sweetness of God and the inner beauty of virtue. But they who utterly despise the world, and strive to live for God under holy discipline, they are not ignorant of God's sweetness promised to those who truly deny themselves, and see more clearly how grievously the world is astray, and in varied ways deceived.

TWENTY-ONE

On Resting in God Above all Gifts and Blessings

1. Above all things, and in all things, you will rest, my soul, in God always, because he is the Saints' everlasting rest. Grant me, sweetest and most loving Jesus, in you to rest above every creature, above all salvation and beauty, above all glory and honour, above all power and dignity, above all knowledge and skilfulness, above all riches and arts, above all gladness and exultation, above all fame and praise, above all sweetness and consolation, above all hope and promising, above all merit and desire, above all gifts and rewards, which you are able to give and pour forth, above all joy and jubilation, which the mind can receive and feel, in a word above all Angels and Archangels and above all the host of heaven; above all things seen and unseen, and above everything which you, God, are not; because you, my Lord God, are best, above all things.

2. You alone are most high, you alone all-powerful, you alone all-sufficient and utterly complete, you alone are all-sweet and all-comforting, you alone are all-noble and all-glorious above all things; in whom all good things at the same time are perfect, always have been, and will be. And that is why it falls short and is insufficient, whatever you give me, apart from yourself, and reveal about yourself or promise, if you yourself are not seen nor fully possessed; for, indeed, my heart cannot truly rest nor be completely content, unless it rest in thee, and transcend all gifts and every creature.

3. O, my beloved spouse, Jesus Christ, purest lover, ruler of all creation, who shall give to me the wings of true freedom, that I may fly and find rest in you? O, when will it be fully given me to be free, and to see how sweet you are, Lord my God? When shall I fully gather myself together in you, that for love I shall not be conscious of myself, but of you alone, beyond all sense and measure, in a way not known to all? But now I often sigh and bear my unhappiness with sorrow, because many evils encounter me in this valley of sufferings, which often disturb me, make me sad and cast a cloud over me, more often hinder me, distract me, allure and entangle, lest I should have free access to you, and enjoy sweet embraces, which are always there for blessed spirits. Let my sighing and manifold desolation on the earth move you.

4. O Jesus, splendour of everlasting glory, solace of my soul on pilgrimage, in your presence my mouth lacks voice and my silence speaks to you. How long does my Lord delay his coming? Let him come to me, his utterly poor one, and make me glad. Let him put out his hand, and snatch the wretched from every anguish. Come, come, because without you there will be no joyous day or hour, because you are my gladness and without you my table is empty. I am wretched and in a manner imprisoned and loaded with fetters, until you restore me with the light of your presence, give me to liberty, and show a loving face.

5. Let others seek something other than you, according to their choice; for my part meanwhile nothing else is pleasing or shall be, but you my God, my hope, eternal salvation. I shall not keep silence, nor cease supplication, until your grace return, and you say to me in my heart:

6. 'Look, I am here, look, I came to you, because you called upon me. Your tears and the longing of your soul, your humiliation and heart's contrition, have inclined me to you, and brought me to you.'

7. And I said: 'Lord, I called on you, and longed to enjoy you, ready for your sake, to reject everything. For you first stirred me to seek you. Be, therefore, blessed, Lord, who wrought this good work upon your servant, according to the multitude of your mercy. What more has your servant to say in your presence, save to humble himself exceedingly before you, ever mindful of his own iniquity and baseness. There is none like you amid all the wonders of heaven and earth. Excellent are your works, your judgments true, and all things are governed by your Providence. Praise, therefore, and glory be to you, Wisdom of the Father. Let my mouth praise and bless you, my soul and all created things together.'

TWENTY-TWO

On Remembering God's Manifold Blessings

1. Lord, open my heart to your law, and teach me to walk in your precepts. Grant me to understand your will, and with great reverence and careful consideration to be mindful of your benefits, both those granted widely and those to me alone, that worthily, after this, I may be fit to render thanks to you. Truly, I know and I confess that I am unable to pay due praise for even the least of your mercies. I am smaller than any of the benefits bestowed on me. And when I think of your majesty, my spirit faints before its greatness.

2. All things which we have in soul and in body, and whatever, outside us or within, naturally or supernaturally we possess, are your benefits, and show you, from whom we receive all good things, to be bountiful, merciful and good. Though one has received more, another less, all, nevertheless, are yours, and without you not the least can be possessed. He who has received greater, cannot boast of his deserving, nor lift himself above others, nor hold the lesser in contempt, because he is the greater and the better who attributes less to himself, and in returning thanks is the more humble and devout. And

he who counts himself cheaper than all, and judges himself more unworthy, is fitter to receive greater.

3. He who has received less must not be saddened, nor take it amiss, nor envy the richer, but rather look to you, and most greatly praise your goodness, because so richly, so freely and generously, 'without respect of persons', you bestow your gifts. All things are from you, and that is why in all things you are to be praised. You know what each one should be given; and why this one should have less and that one more, is not for us but for you to discern, to whom it is clear what each one deserves.

4. That is why, Lord God, I even consider it a great blessing not to have much of that which, outwardly in the opinion of men, may be thought praise and glory; so that each one, his poverty and the worthlessness of his person considered, should not only conceive no grief, or sadness or dejection from it, but rather consolation and great gladness, because you, God, have chosen for yourself, as friends and intimates, the poor and humble and those despised in this world. Your Apostles are themselves witnesses, whom you have made princes over all the earth. Yet they lived in this world without complaint, so humble and gentle, without any malice or guile, that they even 'rejoiced to suffer reproaches for your name', and embraced with joy those things the world hates.

5. Nothing, therefore, should gladden one who loves and knows your benefits, so much as your will in him, and the good pleasure of your everlasting plan, wherein he should find such content and comfort, that he should as readily desire to be the least, as one might wish to be the greatest, and as peaceful and contented in the very last place as in the first,

and as willing to be despised and rejected, even of no name and fame, as others are to be more honoured and greater in the world. For your will and the love of your honour must go before everything, and should console and please him more than all the benefits given, or to be given him.

TWENTY-THREE

On Four Sources of Peace

1. 'Son, now I shall teach you the way of peace and true liberty.'

2. Do, Lord, what you say, because it is pleasing to me to hear this.

3. 'Strive, son, to do another's will rather than your own. Choose always rather to have less than more. Seek always the lower place and to be subject to all. Desire always and pray that the will of God may be completely fulfilled in you. Look, such a man treads the frontiers of peace and rest.'

4. Lord, your brief discourse contains much of perfection in it. Short it is in speech, but full of meaning, and rich in fruit. For if it could be faithfully kept by me, disturbance ought not so easily to arise in me. For as often as I find myself reft of peace and burdened, I discover that I have retreated from this teaching. But you, who can do all things, and cherish always the progress of the soul, grant greater grace that I may be able to fulfil that which you say, and work out my salvation.

5. Lord my God, be not far from me; my God, look to help me, for different thoughts and great fears have risen up against me, afflicting my soul. How shall I pass through unhurt? How shall I break through them?

6. 'I,' he says, 'will go before you, and will make the rough places plain. I will open the prison doors, and reveal to you the hidden secrets.'

7. Do, Lord, as you say, and let all evil thoughts fly before your face. This is my hope and one consolation, to fly to you in every tribulation, to trust in you, from my heart, to call on you, and patiently await your consolation.

A Prayer for the Enlightenment of the Mind

8. Enlighten me, good Jesus, with the brightness of the inner light, and draw out all forms of darkness from the dwelling of my heart. Restrain many wanderings, and shatter the temptations that violently attack. Fight strongly for me, and beat down the evil beasts, lustful allurements, I mean, that peace may be made in your power, and the abundance of your praise may resound in your holy court, that is in a pure conscience. Give commandment to the winds and storms; say to the sea: 'Be still', and to the north wind: 'Blow not'; and there will be a great calm.

9. Send out your light and truth that they may shine through the earth, because I am earth without form and void until you enlighten me. Pour out from above your grace; flood my heart with the dew of heaven; supply the waters of devotion to refresh the face of the earth, and bring forth good and perfect fruit. Lift up my mind, loaded with the mass of my sins, and lift my whole desire to heavenly things, that, with the sweetness of heaven's felicity tasted, it may find no pleasure in thinking of earthly things.

10. Snatch me and deliver me from all the unstable comfort of created things, because no thing created avails fully to still my appetite, and to console. Join me to you by the unbreakable bond of love, because you alone suffice for the one who loves you, and apart from you all other things are trifles.

TWENTY-FOUR

On Avoiding Curiosity on Another's Mode of Living

1. 'Son, do not be inquisitive, and entertain vain cares. What is this or that to you? Follow me. For what is it to you whether he be such or such or another does or says so and so? You have no need to answer for others, but you will give an account of yourself. Why, therefore, entangle yourself? Look, I know all men, and see everything which is done under the sun; and I know how it is with each one, what he thinks, what he wants, and to what end moves his purpose. To me, therefore, everything must be committed; but do you keep yourself in good peace, and leave the restless to be as restless as he will. He shall answer for everything which he shall do or say, because he cannot deceive me.'

2. 'Do not be concerned about the shadow of a great name, nor about the friendship of many, nor about the personal regard of men. For these things beget distractions, and great forms of darkness in the heart. Gladly would I speak my own word to you, and reveal the hidden things, if you would diligently watch for my coming and open the door of your heart to me. Be careful and watchful in prayer, and in all things humble yourself.'

TWENTY-FIVE

On the Basis of the Heart's Stable Peace and True Progress

1. 'Son, I have said: Peace I leave with you, my peace I give to you; not as the world gives, do I give to you. All long for peace, but not all care for that which belongs to true peace. My peace is with the humble and the lowly of heart. Your peace will be in much patience. If you have heard me and followed my voice, you will be able to enjoy much peace.'

2. What, therefore, shall I do, Lord?

3. 'In everything take heed to yourself, what you do, and what you say, and direct all your purpose to this, that you may please me alone, and outside of me desire or seek nothing. But also make no rash judgment about what others say or do, and do not be involved in matters not committed to you, and it may come about that you will be disturbed little or rarely. But never to feel any disturbance, never to suffer any affliction of heart or of body, does not belong to the present time, but is the state of eternal rest. Do not, therefore, conclude that you have found true peace, if you shall feel no grief, nor that all is then good, if you suffer from no enemy, nor this to be perfection, if all things happen according to your desire. And do not then reckon that you are something great, or think that you are specially loved, if you find yourself in a state of great

On Consolation Within 113

ardour or sweetness of spirit, for it is not in such things that the true lover of virtue is known, nor does the progress and perfection of man consist in such things.'

4. In what, then, Lord?

5. 'In offering yourself wholeheartedly to God's will, in not seeking the things which are your own, small or great, in time or in eternity, so that you may remain with the same calm countenance in the rendering of thanks in prosperity and adversity, weighing all things with an even balance. If you shall be so strong and longsuffering in hope, that, if inner consolation is removed, you still prepare your heart for fuller endurance, and do not justify yourself, thinking you ought not to suffer trials so great as these, but rather justify me in all that I ordain, and praise my holiness, then you are walking in the true straight way of peace, and hope will be undoubted that again you will see my face in joy. But if you have come to utter contempt of self, know that then you will enjoy such abundance of peace as is possible where you dwell.'

TWENTY-SIX

On the Excellence of the Free Mind which Devout Prayer Rather than Reading Wins

1. Lord, this is the work of a mature man, never to let his mind slacken from seeking heavenly things, and, among many cares, to move on as if there were no care, not after the fashion of one scarce alive, but by the privilege of a free mind, not clinging to anything created with unmeasured affection.

2. I beg you, my most merciful Lord God, preserve me from the cares of this life, lest I be too involved; from the many needs of the body, lest I be snared by pleasure; from all the obstruction of the soul, lest I be broken by troubles and cast down. I do not mean preserve me from those things which worldly vanity covets with such eagerness, but from those miseries which, by the common curse of mortality, as punishment burden and hold back the soul of your servant, lest it should have strength to enter into the liberty of the spirit, as often as it wish.

3. O my God, unutterable sweetness, turn into bitterness all consolation of the flesh which draws me away from the love of eternal things, and evilly entices me towards itself by setting in my sight some present delight. Let not, my God, let not flesh and blood overcome me, nor the world and its brief glory deceive; let the devil and his cunning not stumble me. Give me strength to resist, patience to endure, constancy to continue on. Give, in place of all the world's consolations, the most sweet anointing of your spirit, and in place of fleshly love, pour into me the love of your name.

4. Look, food, drink, clothing and all other things belonging to the body's poor support, are a burden to the free spirit. Grant that I may use such alleviations with moderation, and not be entangled with desire too great for them. It is not lawful to cast them all aside, because nature must be sustained, but holy law forbids to look for that which goes beyond necessity, and which makes rather for pleasure: for otherwise the flesh would lord it over the spirit. In such matters, I beg, let your hand rule and teach me, that nothing may become too much.

TWENTY-SEVEN

On How a Personal Love Can More Than Anything Hold us Back from Highest Good

1. 'Son, for the whole you must wholly give yourself, and be nothing of your own. Know that love of self harms you more than anything in the world. According to the love and affection which you bear, everything more or less cleaves to you. If your love be pure, sincere and well-ordered, you will not be in bondage to anything. Do not covet what it is not lawful to have; do not wish to have what can hinder you, and rob you of inner liberty. It is a marvel that you do not commit yourself to me from the depths of your heart along with everything which you can desire or possess.'

2. 'Why are you consumed with empty sorrow? Why are you wearied with cares you should not have? Stand by my good pleasure, and you will not suffer loss. If you seek this or that, and want to be here or there, according to your advantage, or the better to fulfil your private pleasure, you will never be at rest or free from anxiety, because some defect will be found in everything, and in every place will be someone to oppose you.'

3. 'It does not, therefore, help to gain or multiply anything externally, but rather in holding it in contempt and utterly rooting it out of the heart. Understand this not only in the matter of money and riches, but also in your aspiration after honour, and longing for empty praise, all of which pass with the world. The place protects little if the spirit of warm devotion is lacking, and that peace sought abroad will not long stand, if the state of your heart is without a true foundation,

that is, unless you shall stand in me, you can change yourself but not improve. For if the opportunity has arisen or been laid hold of, you will find what you fled from or more.'

Prayer for the Purging of the Heart
and for Heavenly Wisdom

4. Make me strong, God, through the grace of your Holy Spirit. Grant me virtue to be made robust in the inner man, and to empty my heart of all useless care and anguish, and not to be drawn by various desires for anything cheap or precious, but to look upon all things as things which pass away, and on myself as destined likewise to pass with them, because there is nothing permanent beneath the sun, where 'all is vanity and vexation of spirit'. O, wise is he who is so minded!

5. Grant me, Lord, heaven's wisdom, that I may learn to seek you above all things and to find you, to relish you above all things and to love, and to understand all other things, as they are, according to your wisdom's ordering of them. Grant me wisely to avoid the flatterer, and patiently to bear an adversary, because this is great wisdom, not to be moved by every wind of words, nor offer an ear to the Siren, wickedly flattering; for so does one go safely on the way begun.

TWENTY-EIGHT

On Slanderers

1. 'Son, do not think it hard if some think ill of you, and say what you are not glad to hear. You should feel worse about yourself, and think no one weaker than you are. If you walk after the spirit, you will not give much weight to words which fly without. It is no small wisdom to keep silent in an evil time, and to turn to me within, and not be troubled by man's judgment.'

2. 'Let your peace be not in the mouth of men. Whether their interpretation of you be for well or for ill, you are not for that reason another man. Where is there true peace and true glory? Is it not in me? And he who has no urge to please men, nor is afraid to displease them, shall enjoy much peace. All disquietude of heart and distraction of the senses, arises from unregulated love or fear.'

TWENTY-NINE

On Calling on God and Blessing Him when Trouble Assails

1. Blessed be your name for ever, Lord, who willed that this temptation and tribulation come upon me. I cannot escape it, but must fly for refuge to you, that you may help me and transform it into good for me. Lord, now I am in tribulation, and it is not well with my heart, but I am much afflicted by what I am now suffering. And now, beloved Father, what shall I say? I am caught in ills which hem me in. 'Save me from this hour? But for this reason I came to this hour', that you might be glorified, when I shall be truly humbled, and set free by you. Let it be your pleasure to deliver me, Lord, for I am poor, and what can I do, and whither go without you. Give patience, Lord, even at this juncture. Help me, my God, and I shall not fear, however greatly burdened I shall be.

2. And now amid these things what shall I do? Lord, thy will be done. I have truly earned to suffer tribulation, and be burdened. And so I must endure, may it be with patience, while the tempest passes, and it becomes better. But potent is your hand, omnipotent to take even this temptation away from me, and soften its impact, that I may not utterly collapse, just as heretofore you have often dealt with me, my God, my mercy. And as much as this is more difficult to me, so much is this 'changing of the right hand of the Most High' easier for you.

THIRTY

On Seeking God's Help and the Certainty of Regaining Grace

1. 'Son, I am the God who comforts in the day of trouble. Come to me, when it is not well with you. This is what chiefly hinders heaven's comfort, that you too slowly turn to prayer. For before you ask me urgently, you seek meanwhile many comforts, and refresh yourself in outer things. And so it comes about that everything is of small avail, until you see that it is I who deliver those who hope in me, and that outside of me there is no real help nor useful counsel, only remedy which does not last. But now, with your spirit revived after the tempest, grow strong again in the light of my mercies, because I am at hand, says the Lord, that I may restore all things, not only as they were, but abundantly, too, and in fuller measure.'

2. 'Is there anything at all difficult to me, and am I like one who says, but does not do? Where is your faith? Stand fast, and carry on. Be longsuffering and a strong man; consolation will come to you at the proper time. Wait for me, wait; I will come and heal you. It is temptation which harasses you, and

empty fear which terrifies. What does anxiety about what may happen in the future bring you, save that you should have sadness upon sadness. Sufficient to the day is its own evil. It is a vain and useless thing to be disturbed or pleased about future things which may never come to pass.'

3. 'But it is the manner of man to be deceived by such imaginings, and it is the mark of a mind which is still weak so lightly to be drawn to the suggestion of the enemy. For he does not care whether by truth or falsehood he deceive and beguile, or whether he brings down by love of what is at hand, or by fear of what may come to pass. Let not your heart be troubled neither let it be afraid. Believe in me and have confidence in my mercy. When you think that you have become remote from me, often I am nearer. When you think that all is nearly lost, often greater gain of merit is at hand. All is not lost when something falls out contrary. You should not judge according to what you feel at the moment, nor so cling to and accept some grief from any quarter befalling, as if all hope of rising above it had been taken away from you.'

4. 'Do not think that you have been utterly abandoned, though, for the moment, I may have sent some tribulation on you, or have even withdrawn some cherished consolation, for this is the way to the kingdom of heaven. And, without doubt, this is more to your advantage, and to that of the rest of my servants, that you should be trained by adversities, than that you should have everything as you would like it. I know your hidden thoughts, and that it is of great advantage for your salvation that at times you should be left without relish, lest you chance to be uplifted in good success, and wish to please yourself in that which you are not. That which I have given I can take away and restore, when it shall please me.'

5. 'When I shall have given, it is mine; when I shall have taken it away, I have not taken what is yours, for mine is every best and perfect gift. If I shall have sent you grief or any form of opposition, do not be angry, nor let your heart be daunted; I am able quickly to uplift, and transform every burden into joy. Notwithstanding, I am just and much to be praised when I do this with you.'

6. 'If you think rightly and observe truthfully, you should never be so deeply saddened by adversity, but rather rejoice and be thankful, indeed, to count this special joy that, afflicting you with sorrows, I do not spare you. Just as the Father loved me, so I love you, I said to my beloved disciples, whom, assuredly, I did not send forth to earthly joys, but to great conflicts; not to honours, but to manifold contempt; not to leisure but to toils; not to rest, but to the bearing of much fruit in patience. These words, my son, remember.'

THIRTY-ONE

*On Neglecting all Things Created that
the Creator may be Found*

1. Lord, I still stand in need of greater grace, if I am to reach that point where no one and no thing created shall avail to hinder me. For so long as anything holds me back, I am unable freely to fly to you. He wished to fly freely who said: 'Who will give me wings like a dove, and I will fly and be at rest?' What is more peaceful than the 'single eye'? And what more free than one who desires nothing upon earth? Therefore must a man rise over everything created and utterly abandon himself, and stand in ecstasy of mind, and see that you, the creator of all things, have nothing in common with the things created. And unless a man be set free from everything created, he will not be able freely to reach to things divine. For this is the reason why few are found who give themselves to contemplation, because few know how to separate themselves fully from created things, which are doomed to perish.

2. For this great grace is needed, to uplift the soul and snatch it higher than its own self. And unless a man be uplifted in spirit, and freed from everything created, and totally united to God, whatever he knows, whatever, too, he has, is of no great weight. He will long be small, and lie low beneath, who counts anything great, but the only one, immense, eternal good. And whatever God is not, is nothing, and must be reckoned nothing. There is a great difference between the wisdom of an enlightened and devout man, and the knowledge of an educated and studious cleric. Much nobler is that teaching which distils from God's influence above, than that which is toilsomely won by man's intelligence.

3. There are many found who long for contemplation, but take no pains to practise what is required for it. It is a great hindrance, too, that signs and things of sense are regarded, with little thought of utter dying to oneself. I do not know what it is, and by what spirit we are led, and what we are aiming at, that we who are, it seems, called 'spiritual', devote so much toil and deeper anxiety to cheap and ephemeral things, and scarcely ever, with our senses fully mobilised, think about our inner selves.

4. The sorrow of it! – we remember for a little time, and forthwith break out again, nor weigh that which we do with careful scrutiny. We do not give attention to where our feelings lie, and do not grieve that all we have and are, is defiled. All flesh, indeed, had gone the way of corruption, and that is

why the great deluge followed. Since, then, our inner feelings are much corrupted, it follows that the action which results, and which reveals the lack of inner strength, should also be corrupted. From a pure heart comes the fruit of a good life.

5. How much a man has done, is the question, but not such weighty thought is taken as to how great the worth from which he acts. Attention is given to whether he be valiant, rich, handsome, clever, or a good writer, a good singer, a good workman; how poor in spirit he is, how patient, gentle, how devout and spiritual, is not mentioned by many. Nature looks on the outward appearance of a man, grace has regard to what is within. The former is commonly mistaken; the latter hopes in God, so that it be not deceived.

THIRTY-TWO

On Self-denial and the Abandonment of all Desire

1. 'Son, you cannot possess perfect liberty unless you completely renounce your own self. They are shackled, all people of property, lovers of themselves, covetous, anxious, restless folk, seekers of luxuries rather than the things of Christ, always planning and setting up that which will not stand. For all will perish, which has not sprung from God. Hold fast this short, inclusive saying: Abandon all, and you will find all; give up desire, and you will discover rest. Ponder this in your mind, and when you have fulfilled it, you will understand everything.'

2. Lord, this is not the burden of one day, nor a game for little children; indeed in this short saying, is included all the perfection of the truly godly.

3. 'Son, you must not be turned away or immediately discouraged, because you have heard the way of the perfect, but rather be challenged to higher paths, or at least to aspire for them with longing. Would that it were thus with you, and you had reached this point, that you should be no longer a lover of yourself, but should stand simply ready for my nod and his whom I have set before you, the Father's. Then you would truly please me, and all your life would pass in joy and peace. You have still much to renounce, things which, unless you resign them absolutely to me, you will not win that which you ask. I counsel you to buy of me gold tried in the fire that you may be rich, that is heavenly wisdom, which treads down all base things. Put aside earthly wisdom, all things which are pleasing to men at large, and to yourself.'

4. 'I have said that cheaper things must be bought by you instead of those things held precious among men and of high esteem. For wondrous cheap, and small and almost abandoned to forgetfulness, seems true heavenly wisdom, which is not highly wise in its own eyes and seeks no earthly glory, the wisdom which many honour with their lips, but in their life are far from assenting to it; yet it is the pearl of great price, hidden away from many.'

THIRTY-THREE

*On the Heart's Inconstancy and
Directing the Final Aim to God*

1. 'Son, do not trust your feelings; that which now is will be quickly changed into something else. As long as you shall live, you are subject to change, even though you wish it not, so that you are found now joyful, now sad, now at peace, now disturbed, now devout, now not devout, now zealous, now careless, now solemn, now light-hearted. But the man who is wise and well-taught in the spirit stands above these things, not paying attention to what he feels, or from what quarter the wind of instability may blow, but that the whole drive of his mind should make progress towards the proper and desired end. For so will he be able to remain one and the same man, unshaken, with the single eye of his desire, fixed unflinchingly, through the manifold changes of circumstance, on me.'

2. 'But the purer the eye of desire shall be, by so much will progress be more steadfast through the changeful gales. But in many the eye of pure desire grows dim; for a look is quickly cast back at something delightsome which befalls, and rarely is one found completely free from the blemish of self-seeking. So once the Jews came to Bethany to Martha and Mary, not only on account of Jesus, but to see Lazarus. The eye, therefore, of desire must be purified, so that it be single and straight, directed towards me, beyond all those different things which lie between.'

THIRTY-FOUR

On God's Supreme Sweetness in All Things to those that Love Him

1. Look, my God and my all. What more do I wish for, what more happily can I desire? O, delightful and sweet word! But to the one who loves the Word, and not the world, and those things which are in the world, God and all things are mine. To one who understands, sufficient has been said, and often to repeat it is pleasing for one who loves. Indeed, when you

are present, everything is pleasant; but when you are absent, everything disgusts. You still the heart, and give great peace and festal gladness. You make us think as we should think, on all matters, and in all to praise you, nor without you can anything long please, but if it is to be pleasing and of good savour, your grace must be there, and it must be spiced with the spice of your wisdom.

2. To whom you give relish, what will not be truly tasty to him? And to whom you give not relish, what will be able to bring pleasure to him? But the wise in the world, and those who savour the flesh, fall short in your wisdom, for in those is found utter vanity, and in these death. But those who, by contempt for worldly things, and by making dead the flesh, follow you, are recognised as truly wise, for they are translated from vanity to truth, from the flesh to the spirit. They taste that God is good, and whatever good is found in things created, they ascribe the whole of the praise of its creator. Yet unlike, unlike indeed, is the enjoyment of the creator to the enjoyment of that which he creates, as unlike as eternity and time, uncreated light and light reflected.

3. O, eternal light, transcending all lights created, darting down your lightnings from on high, and penetrating the deep recesses of my heart! Make pure, joyous, enlightened and alive my spirit, that with all its powers, and with joy beyond all bounds, it may cleave to you. O, when will come that blessed and longed-for hour, when you will satisfy me with your presence, and be to me all in all? So long as this remains withheld, joy will not be full. Still (alas, the sorrow!) the 'old man' still lives in me; he is not wholly crucified, nor utterly dead; he still lusts strongly against the spirit, stirs civil war, nor suffers the rule of the soul to be tranquil.

4. But you who control the power of the sea, and still the surge of its waves, rise up, aid me. Scatter the peoples who seek war. Crush them by your might. Show forth, I beg, your mighty works, and let your right hand be glorified, for there is no other hope or refuge for me save in you, Lord, my God.

THIRTY-FIVE

On the Impossibility of Escaping Temptation in This Life

1. 'Son, you are never safe in this life, but as long as you shall live the armour of the spirit is essential for you. You live among enemies and are embattled on the right and left. If, therefore, you do not use on all sides the shield of endurance, you will not go long unwounded. Above all, if you do not set your heart firmly upon me, with true willingness to bear everything for me, you will be unable to sustain that hot attack, nor to reach the palm of the blessed. Therefore you must struggle manfully right through, and use a strong hand against those things which stand in your way. For to him who conquers, the manna is given, and to the slothful wretchedness is left.'

2. 'If you seek peace in this life, how then will you reach eternal peace? Do not prepare yourself for much rest, but for great endurance. Seek true peace, not on earth, but in heaven, not in men, nor in other things created, but in God alone. For the love of God you must undergo all things gladly, toils, undoubtedly, and sorrows, temptations, harassments, anxieties, compulsions, weaknesses, injuries, insults, reproaches, humiliations, confusions, rebukes and despisings. These help towards virtue, these test Christ's recruit, these

On Consolation Within 127

weave a heavenly crown. I will duly pay eternal recompense for brief toil, and glory without end for passing shame.'

3. 'Do you think that you will always have spiritual consolations according as you wish? My Saints did not always have such, but many griefs and manifold temptations, and great desolations. But they patiently upheld themselves in all things, and trusted more in God than in themselves, knowing that the sufferings of the present time are not to be compared with the glory to be won. Do you wish to have at once what many, after many tears and great toils, scarce obtained? Wait on the Lord, play the man and be strong; do not despair, nor abandon your post, but constantly, for God's glory, expose body and soul. I will plenteously repay, and will be with you in every trouble.'

THIRTY-SIX

On the Empty Judgments of Men

1. 'Son, anchor your soul firmly in the Lord, and fear no human judgment, when conscience pronounces you trusty and innocent. It is good and blessed to suffer in such fashion, and this will not be grievous to the humble heart, and to one who trusts in God rather than in himself. Many men have many things to say, and therefore little credence is called for. And, moreover, it is not possible to please everybody. Although Paul was zealous to please all men in the Lord, and became all things to all men, yet he also held it of very small account that he should be judged by man.'

2. 'He did enough for the upbuilding and salvation of others, as far as in him lay, and he was able; but he was not able to

avoid being judged at times and despised by others. And so he committed all to God, who knew all, and with patience and humility defended himself against the tongues of those who spoke evil, and also those who thought folly and falsehood, and who at their caprice, made accusations. Yet he sometimes answered them, lest from his silence scandal should arise for the weak.'

3. 'Who are you that should be afraid of mortal man? He is today, and tomorrow will not appear. Fear God, and do not quail before the terrors of men. What can anyone do against you by words or violence? He rather hurts himself than you; nor will he be able to escape the judgment of God, whoever he is. Keep God before your eyes, and do not strive with querulous words. But if for the moment you seem to go under and to suffer shame unmerited, do not be put out by this, and by impatience diminish your crown, but rather look heavenwards to me, who am able to snatch you from all pain and injury and to render to each person according to his works.'

THIRTY-SEVEN

On Liberty of Heart to be Won by Pure Complete Self-surrender

1. 'Son, abandon yourself and you will find me. Stand without choice or any sort of ownership, and you will always gain. For greater grace will be added to you, as soon as you shall renounce yourself, and take yourself not back again.'

2. Lord, how many times shall I renounce myself and in what things abandon myself?

3. 'Always, and at every hour; as in small things, so in great. I make no exception, but want you to be found stripped in all things. Otherwise, how will you be able to be mine, and I yours, unless, within and without, you are denuded of all will of your own? The quicker you do this, so much the better it will be with you, and the more fully and sincerely, and so much more will you please me, and be more abundantly rewarded.'

4. Some renounce themselves but only with some exception, for they do not fully trust God, and give attention to providing for themselves. Some, too, offer everything at first, but later, when temptation strikes, they return to their own devices, and so make very small progress in virtue. These will not reach the true freedom of a pure heart, and the grace of joyous fellowship with me, unless there has first been made complete renunciation, and a daily putting of self to death, without which fruitful union stands not, nor will stand.'

5. 'I have most frequently said to you what now I say again: Abandon yourself, renounce yourself, and you will enjoy great peace within. Give the whole for the whole; demand nothing, seek nothing in return; stand simply and unhesitatingly in me, and you will possess me. You will be free in heart, and darkness shall not overwhelm you. Strive for this, pray for this, long for this, that you be despoiled of all ownership, and, possessing nothing, follow Jesus, who had nothing, so as to die to yourself and live eternally for me. Then all empty fancies will fade away, all evil disturbances and superfluous cares. Then, too, fear beyond measure shall retreat, and love that should not be shall die.'

THIRTY-EIGHT

On the Good Management of Outward
Things and Recourse to God

1. 'Son, you must diligently press towards this that, in every place, action, or business with things outside, you are free within and in control of yourself, with all things subjected to you, not you to them; that you be master and director of your actions, not servant, nor hireling, but rather a freeman and a true Hebrew, entering into the lot and liberty of God's children, who stand above the present, their eyes upon eternity, who with their left eye look on passing things, and with their right on heavenly; whom temporal things draw not to entwine, but rather do they themselves draw temporal things to do good service, just as they were set in place and order to do by God, the supreme workman, who has left nothing without a proper place in his creation.'

2. 'But if, in every circumstance, you take your stand, not in outward appearance, nor scan with carnal eye things seen and heard, but immediately, like Moses, enter the tabernacle to take God's counsel, you will often hear God's reply and return instructed about much of that which is and is yet to be. For Moses often had recourse to the tabernacle to find the answer to doubts and questionings, and fled to the aid of prayer, to be delivered from dangers and the depravities of men. And so you must fly to the secret place of your heart, begging earnestly God's succour. For this was why Joshua, and the sons of Israel, were deceived, it is said, by the men of Gibeon, because they did not inquire of the mouth of the Lord, but, too credulous, were deluded by pleasant speech and false piety.'

THIRTY-NINE

On Avoidance of Preoccupation with Business

1. 'Son, always commit your cause to me. At its proper time I will dispose of it aright. Wait for my ordering, and you will know profit therefrom.'

2. Lord, gladly enough I commit all things to you, for my planning profits little. Would that I did not cling so much to future contingencies, but unhesitatingly offered myself to your good pleasure.

3. 'Son, a man often strives hard for something he covets, but when he has secured it, his feelings change, because they do not cohere strongly round the same object, but thrust a man from one thing to another. Therefore self-renunciation is not a trifling thing – even in trifles.'

4. 'A man's true progress lies in self-denial, and the man who has denied himself is truly free and safe. But the old enemy, opposing everything good, does not cease from tempting, but day and night devises grievous ambush, if perchance he can tumble the unwary into the snare of deception. Watch and pray, lest you fall into temptation, says the Lord.'

FORTY

On Man's Lack of Personal Goodness in which to Boast

1. 'Lord, what is man that you are mindful of him, or the Son of man that you visit him?' What has man deserved that you should grant him your grace? Lord, of what can I complain, if you desert me? Or what justly can I plead, if you have not done as I desire? Surely this I can in truth consider, and say: Lord I am nothing, I can do nothing, I have nothing good in myself, but in all things fall short and always tend to nothing. And unless I had been helped by you, and shaped within by you, I am made wholly lukewarm and remiss.

2. But you, Lord, are yourself always the same, and endure forever, always good, just and holy, doing all things well, in just and holy fashion, and ordering them in wisdom. But I, who am more prone to failure than to progress, do not always continue in the same condition, because changes sevenfold pass over me. But all is quickly made better, when it pleases you, and you have stretched forth your helping hand, because you alone, without man's assent, can so bring succour, and in such measure strengthen, that my face is no more changed to turn the other way, but in you alone my transformed heart finds rest.

3. And so, if I knew well how to cast aside all human consolation, whether to win devotion, or because of the constraint I am under to seek you, since there is no man to console me, then could I deservedly hope in your grace, and rejoice in the gift of new consolation.

4. Thanks be to you from whom all comes, whenever it goes well with me. But I am vanity and nothing in your sight, an inconstant weakling. Whence, then, can I boast, or on what grounds covet reputation? Indeed, of my nothingness? And utterly vain is that. Truly, empty glory is an evil plague, the greatest vanity, because it draws us from true glory and robs us of heaven's grace. For while a man pleases himself he displeases you; while he pants after the praises of man, he is deprived of true virtues.

5. But it is true glory and holy exultation to glory in you, and not in self, to rejoice in your name, and not in one's own worth, and not to delight in any created thing, save on your account. Let your name be praised, not mine; let your work be magnified, not mine; let your holy name be blessed, but let nothing be attributed to me from the praises of men. You are my glory, you the exultation of my heart. In you shall I glory, and exult all day, but of myself I shall boast of nothing, save of my infirmities.

6. Let the Jews seek the honour 'which comes from one another'; that shall I covet 'which is from God alone'. Indeed every human glory, every temporal honour, all worldly exaltation, set beside your eternal glory is vanity and folly. O, my Truth and my Mercy, my God, blessed Trinity, to you alone be praise, honour, virtue and glory for ever and ever.

FORTY-ONE

On Contempt for all Worldly Honour

1. 'Son, do not take it to yourself if you see others honoured and uplifted, while you are despised and humiliated. Lift up your heart to me in heaven, and the contempt of men on earth will not make you sad.'

2. Lord, we are blind, and quickly seduced by vanity. If I see myself aright, never was harm done to me by anything created so that I have no just complaint against you. But because I have often, and gravely sinned against you, deservedly is everything created in arms against me. To me, therefore, shame and contempt are justly due, but to you praise, honour and glory. And unless I shall have prepared myself for this, to wit, that I gladly accept that every creature despise and abandon me, and that I should be held for absolutely nothing, I cannot be brought to peace and firm strength within, nor be spiritually enlightened, and fully united to you.

FORTY-TWO

On the Fact that Peace Cannot be Found in Men

1. 'Son, if you let your peace depend on any person on account of your opinion of him or familiarity, you will be unstable and entangled. But if you betake yourself to the ever living and abiding truth, the desertion or death of a friend will not make you sad. In me the love of a friend should stand, and for my sake he is to be esteemed, whoever has seemed good to you and very dear in this life. Without me friendship is neither strong nor lasting, nor is that love true and pure, which I do not unite. You should be so dead to the affections of those you love, that, as far as in you lies, you would choose to be without any human fellowship. In proportion as a man draws nearer to God, so the further he withdraws from all earthly solace. And the higher he climbs towards God, so the deeper he descends in himself, and the cheaper he becomes in his own eyes.

2. Whoever ascribes anything to himself, blocks the pathway for the grace of God, because the grace of the Holy Spirit always seeks the humble heart. If you knew how to make yourself utterly nothing, and to empty yourself of all human love, then it would be mine to pour myself into you with great grace. When you look to things created, then the view of the Creator is withdrawn from you. Learn in all things for his sake to subdue yourself; then you will be strong enough to

attain to the knowledge of God. However small it may be, if anything is loved and regarded beyond due measure, it holds one back from the highest, and corrupts.'

FORTY-THREE

On the Emptiness of Worldly Knowledge

1. 'Son, let not the fair and subtle words of men influence you. For the kingdom of God is not in speech but in virtue. Give ear to my words, for they fire the heart and lighten the mind, they bring contrition, and supply manifold consolation. Never read a word that you may appear more learned or more wise. Give heed to the destruction of your vices, because this will be to your fuller advantage than the knowledge of many difficult questions.'

2. 'Much though you may have read and understood, you must always come back to the one first principle: I am he who teaches man knowledge, and to little ones I give clearer understanding than can be taught by man. He to whom I speak will be quickly wise, and will advance much in spirit. Alas for those who seek after much abstruse knowledge from men, and give small care about how to serve me. The time will come when Christ, the master of masters, will come, the Lord of Angels, to hear the lessons of everyone, and to examine each one's conscience. And then will he search Jerusalem with lanterns, and the hidden things of darkness will be revealed, and the arguings of speech shall fall silent.'

3. 'I am he who in a moment lifts the humble mind, so that it may grasp more reasonings of eternal truth, than if it had studied ten years in the schools. I teach without the din of words, the chaos of opinions, the arrogance of honour, the

136 *The Imitation of Christ*

strife of arguments. I am he who teaches to despise the things of earth, to seek those of eternity and savour them, to fly from honours, endure offences, to place all hope in me, to want nothing apart from me, and, above all, to love me fervently.'

4. 'For there was one who, by loving me deeply, learned things divine, and spoke words of wonder. He advanced more by abandoning all things, than by the study of subtleties. But to some I speak of ordinary matters, to some of matters peculiar to themselves; to some I show myself gently in signs and symbols, but for some, in bright light, I unveil mysteries. There is the voice of books, but it does not instruct all alike, because I am the teacher of truth within, the examiner of the heart, the discerner of thoughts, the prompter of deeds, dividing to each as I shall judge appropriate.'

FORTY-FOUR

On Meddling with that which does not Concern us

1. 'Son, in many matters you should be ignorant, and count yourself dead on earth, and one to whom the whole world has been crucified. Many things, too, you should pass by with a deaf ear, and think more of that which pertains to your peace. It is more useful to turn your eyes away from that which displeases, and to leave to each man his own opinion, than to be subjected to the arguments of controversy. If you stand well with God, and look to his judgment, you will more easily bear being beaten.'

2. O Lord, to what have we come? Look, a temporal loss is mourned over, and for a small gain there is toil and hurry, and spiritual damage slips away into forgetfulness, and is

scarcely thought about again. Thought is given to that which is of small or no advantage; and what is in the highest degree needful, is passed negligently by, because the whole person flows down into outward things, and unless it quickly comes to itself again, lies willingly in outward things.

FORTY-FIVE

On not Believing Everyone and How Easily We Slip in Speech

1. Grant me help, Lord, in tribulation, for vain is the aid of man. How often have I not found faith there, where I thought to possess it! How often, too, have I found it, where I less expected to do so! Vain, therefore, is hope in men, but the salvation of the just is in you, God. Be blessed, O Lord, my God, in all things which happen to us. We are weak and unstable, quickly we are deceived and changed.

2. Who is the man who is able so warily and circumspectly to guard himself, that he does not fall into some deception and perplexity? But he who trusts in you, Lord, and seeks you from a heart unfeigned, does not slip so easily. And if he falls into some tribulation, in whatever fashion, too, he may have been tangled, he will quickly be rescued by you, or by you consoled, because you do not desert the one who hopes in you to the end. A faithful friend who carries on through all his friend's harassments, is not often found. You, Lord, you alone are utterly faithful in everything, and there is not another such beside you.

3. O how truly wise was that holy soul who said: 'My mind is established and founded in Christ.' If it should be so with

me, the fear of man would not so easily dismay me, nor the javelins of man's words move me. Who is sufficient to foresee all things, who to guard against ills yet to come? Even if foreseen, they still often hurt; what can things unforeseen do, but gravely wound us. But why have I not better provided for my wretched self? Why, too, have I so readily trusted others? But we are men, and nothing more than frail men, although we are counted and called angels by some. Whom shall I trust, Lord, whom trust but you? You are truth which does not deceive, nor can deceive. And again: 'Every man is a liar,' weak, inconstant and fallible, especially in speech, so that which seems, on the face of it to ring true, should not immediately be believed.

4. How wisely you have warned us beforehand to beware of men, and that 'a man's foes are those of his own household'; and that he should not be believed who has said: 'He is here, or he is there.' I have been instructed, at cost to myself, I hope to my greater caution, and not to folly. 'Be wary,' says someone, 'be wary, keep to yourself what I say.' And while I keep silent and think it hidden with me, he, on his part, cannot keep silent about what he said should be kept unsaid, forthwith betrays me and himself, and is gone. From speech so mischievous and such reckless men, protect me, Lord, lest I fall into their hands, and may I never commit such sins. Grant that the word on my lips be true and steadfast, and remove far from me a deceitful tongue. I must in every way guard against that which I do not wish to suffer.

5. O how good it is and fraught with peace to keep silent about others, nor believe everything without distinction, nor lightly pass it on, to reveal oneself to few, and to seek you ever as the discerner of the heart, and not to be carried round by

every wind of words, but to pray that all things, within and without, be done according to the good pleasure of your will. How safe for the conservation of heaven's grace it is to fly from the outward show of man, nor to covet what seems to call for public admiration, but to pursue with total earnestness those things which bring amendment of life and warm zeal! How many has virtue, made known and in untimely fashion praised, harmed! How healthily has grace, kept in silence in this frail life, which is said to be all temptation and warfare, brought profit.

FORTY-SIX

On Trusting God when the Shafts of Words are Flying

1. 'Son, stand firm and hope in me. For what are words but words? They fly through the air, but do not hurt a stone. If you are guilty, think how gladly you would amend yourself. If nothing is on your conscience, consider that you would willingly bear this for God. Little enough it is that you sometimes bear even words, you who are not yet able to endure hard blows. Why do such trifles go to your heart, save that you are still carnal, and pay more attention to men than you should? For because you fear to be despised you do not wish to be blamed for your transgressions and seek the poor shelter of excuses.'

2. 'But examine yourself better and you will recognise that the impure and empty love of pleasing men still lives in you. For when you run away from being abased and confounded for your faults, it is assuredly clear that you are neither a truly humble man, nor truly dead to the world, and the world not crucified for you. But listen to my word, and you will not care for ten thousand words of men. Look, if everything

should be said against you, which can be most maliciously imagined, what harm could they do if you let them all pass right through, and considered them no more than a fragment of chaff? Could they pluck out even one hair?'

3. 'But he who has no heart inside him, nor God before his eyes, is easily stirred by a word of censure. But he who trusts in me, nor desires to stand by his own judgment, is beyond the fear of men. For I am judge and discerner of all secrets. I know in what manner a thing is done, I know the one who does the injury and the one who bears it. That word went out from me, and by my permission this happened, that the thoughts of many hearts might be revealed. I will judge the guilty and the innocent, but beforehand I have willed to try them both by secret judgment.'

4. 'The witness of men is often false. My judgment is true, will stand and not be overturned. For the most part it lies hidden, and to few is it open in all details; yet it never errs, nor can, though to the eyes of fools it seems not right. Recourse, then, must be had to me in all judgment, and there must be no leaning on one's own opinion. For the just man shall not be confounded, whatever has befallen him from God. Even if some unjust charge shall be preferred against him, he will not greatly care; nor will he vainly exult if through others he be reasonably shown to be innocent. For he always considers that I am he who tries the heart and the reins, who judges not according to the countenance and the outward appearance of man. For often in my eyes that is discovered blameworthy which, in man's judgment, is believed worthy of praise.'

5. Lord God, just judge, strong and patient, who know the frailty and depravity of man, be my strength and all my

confidence, for my conscience is not enough for me. You know what I do not know. And so, under all blame, I should humble myself and meekly endure it. Pardon me, therefore, of your grace, as often as I have not acted thus, and grant me, the next time, the grace of greater endurance. For your abundant mercy is better for my winning of your pardon, than the justice, which I imagine I possess, for defence against the conscience which lies in wait for me. And if I am conscious of no sin, yet in this I cannot justify myself, for if your mercy be removed, no man living shall be justified in your sight.

FORTY-SEVEN

On Bearing Burdens to Win Eternal Life

1. 'Son, let not the labours which you have taken up for me break you, nor let tribulations in any way cast you down; but let my promise in every situation strengthen and comfort you. I am sufficient to repay beyond all bourne and measure. You will not long labour here, nor for ever be burdened with sorrows. Wait a little while, and you will see a swift end of evils. One hour will come when all toil and turmoil shall cease. Little and short is all that passes with time.'

2. 'Do diligently what you do; toil faithfully in my vineyard; I will be your wages. Write, read, sing, weep, be silent, pray, endure adversities manfully; eternal life is worth all these conflicts and greater. Peace will come on one day, which is known to the Lord. And it will be neither day nor night, as we know it at this time, but light unending, brightness without end, established peace, and carefree rest. You will not then say: Who shall deliver me from the body of this death? Nor will you cry: Alas for me, because my sojourning is prolonged, because death shall be hurled down, salvation shall not fail, there will be no anxiety, blessed joy, sweet and beauteous fellowship.'

3. 'O, if you had but seen the everlasting crowns of the Saints in heaven, with what glory they now exult, they who once in this world were held in contempt and considered unworthy of life itself, truly you would humble yourself even to the earth, and would strive to subject yourself to all, rather than to be set over a single one; nor would you covet this life's happy days, but would rather rejoice to suffer tribulation for God, and would consider it greatest gain to be counted nothing among men.'

4. 'O, if these things tasted sweet to you and penetrated deep into your heart, how would you dare to make even one complaint? Are not all toilsome things to be endured for eternal life? To lose or to gain the kingdom of God is no small matter. Lift, therefore, your face heavenward. Look, I and all my Saints along with me, who in this world had great strife, now rejoice, now are comforted, now are beyond care, now rest, and will abide with me for ever in my Father's kingdom.'

FORTY-EIGHT

On Eternity And The Troubles of This Life

1. O, most blessed dwelling-place of Heaven's realm! O, day most bright of eternity, which night does not darken, and highest truth forever shines upon; day always glad, always beyond care, and never changing for the contrary! O, would that day had shone forth, and all these things of time had met their end! Indeed upon the Saints it shines forever with

glorious brightness, but only from afar, and as if in a mirror, for those on earthly pilgrimage.

2. The citizens of heaven know how joyous that day is. The exiled sons of Eve sigh because this day is bitter and wearisome. The days of this time are few and evil, full of sorrows and pressing trials; where a man is soiled by many sins, snared by many passions, shackled by many fears, torn apart by many cares, distracted by many questionings, tangled with worthless things, crowded round by many errors, worn by many toils, burdened by temptations, weakened by pleasures and tortured by want.

3. O, when will there be an end of these evils? When shall I be freed from the wretched servitude of vice? When shall I be mindful of you, Lord, alone? When shall I be without any hindrance in true liberty, without any thing to weigh down mind and body? When will there be peace well-founded, peace beyond disturbance and care, peace within and without, peace on all sides established? Good Jesus, when shall I stand to look upon you? When shall I gaze upon the glory of your kingdom? When will you be all in all to me? O, when shall I be with you in your kingdom, which you have prepared for those that love you from eternity? I am left a poor exile on hostile soil amid daily wars and the direst misfortunes.

4. Comfort my exile, lessen my sorrow, because all my longing pants for you. For whatever solace this world offers is all a burden to me. I want to enjoy you deeply, but I am not able to lay hold of it. I want to hold fast to heavenly things but the things of time, and passions not put to death, press me down. In my mind I wish to be above all things, but in the flesh I am forced against my will to be beneath. And so, unhappy man,

I battle with myself, and am made a burden to myself, while the spirit strives upward and the flesh down.

5. O, what I suffer within, while with my mind I think of heavenly things, and straightway a rout of carnal temptations and thoughts rush upon me as I pray! 'My God, be not far from me, nor turn away in anger from your servant. Flash forth your lightning and scatter them. Loose your arrows', and let all the enemy's imaginings be confounded. Gather again my senses to yourself. Make me forget all worldly things. Grant me quickly to cast off and despise the imaginations of sin. Help me, eternal truth, that no vanity may move me. Come, heavenly sweetness, and let all impurity flee from your face. Forgive me, too, and in mercy deal gently with me, whenever in prayer I think of anything but you. For I confess in truth that I am commonly distracted. For again and again I am not there where I stand or sit, but rather where I am carried by my thoughts. I am there, where my thought is. And my thought is often there where what I love is. Often there comes into my mind what naturally delights, or what from habit pleases.

6. That is why you, eternal Truth, said plainly: 'Where your treasure is, there your heart is, too.' If I love heaven, I gladly think about heavenly things. If I love the world, I rejoice with the world's delights, and am saddened by its adversities. If I love the flesh, I often imagine those things which belong to the flesh. If I love the spirit, I delight to think of spiritual things. For whatever things I love, about those I gladly speak and hear, and I carry home with me the mental pictures of such things. But happy is that man, who, for your sake, Lord, permits all created things to leave him, who does violence to nature, and crucifies the lusts of the flesh by the fervour of the spirit, and with his conscience serene, makes pure prayer to you, and is worthy to find place in the angelic choirs, with all things worldly, outward and inward, banished.

FORTY-NINE

On the Longing For Eternal Life, and the Greatness of the Rewards Promised to those who Strive

1. 'Son, when you feel the longing for eternal blessedness being poured into you from above, and eagerly desire to depart from the frail dwelling of the body, that you may be able to gaze upon my splendour without shadow of turning, open wide your heart and lay hold of this sacred aspiration. Return the most abundant thanks to heaven's goodness which so courteously deals with you, mercifully visits you, warmly stirs, powerfully uplifts, lest by your own weight you slip to earthly things. For you do not receive this from your own thought or effort, but only by the courtesy of heaven's grace and God's regard, in order that you may advance in virtues and greater humility, and fit yourself for conflicts yet to be, and that you may be zealous to cling to me with all your heart's affection, and with fervent will strive to serve.'

2. 'Son, often the fire burns, but the flame does not rise without smoke. And so, with some, longings for heaven blaze up, and yet they are not free from the feelings of the flesh. That is why it is not with completely unmixed motives that they act for God's glory, when they pray so earnestly to him. Of such sort, too, is often your longing, which you have made out to be so urgent. For that is not pure and perfect, which is tainted with your own convenience.'

3. 'Seek, not what is delightsome and advantageous to yourself, but what is acceptable to me and brings me honour. For if you judge aright you must set what I ordain before your own longing, and everything which can be its object, and follow it. You might wish now to be in the glorious liberty of the children of God; the eternal dwelling place, and heavenly fatherland full of joy already delights you, but that hour has not yet come, but there is yet another time, yes, a time of war, of toil and testing. You desire to be filled with highest good, but you cannot attain it immediately. I am it; await for me, says the Lord, till the kingdom of God comes.'

4. 'You are still to be tried on earth and trained in many things. Sometimes encouragement will be given you, but abundant satisfaction shall not be granted. Be strong, therefore, and stalwart to do, as well as to endure, that which runs counter to nature. You must put on the new man, and be changed into another person. You must often do what you do not want to do, and often give up what you wish. What pleases others will make progress; what pleases you will halt short. What others say will be heard; what you say will be counted nothing. Others will ask and receive; you will ask and not gain what you ask.'

5. 'Others will be great on the lips of men, but about you nothing will be said. To others this or that will be entrusted, but you will be judged useful for nothing. On account of this nature will at times be saddened, and greatly if you will bear it silently. In these and similar ways the faithful servant of the Lord is commonly tried, in such fashion that he may be able to deny and break himself in all things. There is scarcely anything of the sort in which you need so much to die, as in seeing and bearing what runs counter to your will, but most of all when things which are inexpedient, and seem less than useful to you, are the subject of commandment. And because you do not dare to resist a higher authority, placed, as you are, under authority, for that reason it seems hard to you to walk at the nod of another, and to forego what you feel yourself.'

6. 'But consider, son, the fruit of these labours, the swift end and the reward exceeding great, and you do not find them a burden, but the strongest solace for your endurance. For, in return for this trifling wilfulness, which you now freely abandon, in heaven you will always have your desire fulfilled. There, indeed, you will find everything you have wished, everything you will be able to desire. There you will have the power to do all good with no fear of losing it. There your will, at one always with me, will want nothing outside of me, or belonging to yourself. There no one will withstand you, complain about you, or frustrate you, and nothing will block your way, but all things you have longed for will be at hand together, will refresh your whole desiring, and fill it to the very brim. There I will give glory in return for scorn endured, the garment of praise for sorrow, for the lowest place a seat in the kingdom for ever. There will be manifest the fruit of obedience, the toil of penitence will rejoice, and humble submission will be gloriously crowned.'

7. 'Now, therefore, bow yourself humbly under the hands of all men, and do not let anyone's words or commands trouble you. But let this be your chief care that, whether it be your Superior, a lesser person or an equal who had required anything from you or hinted as much, you receive it all for good, and with a sincere will strive to do fully what is asked. Let one seek this, another that, let this man boast in this, another in that, and be praised a thousand thousand times, but do you take joy neither in this nor that but only in despising yourself, and in my good pleasure and honour only. This must be your aspiration, that God be ever glorified in you, be it in life or death.'

FIFTY

On the Need for a Forsaken Man to Commit Himself to God

1. Lord God, Holy Father, be now and forever blessed, because as you wish, so it has been done, and what you do is good. Let your servant rejoice in you and not in himself, nor in any other, because you alone are true joy, you are my hope and my crown, you are my joy and honour, Lord. What has your servant save what he has received of you, even without his deserving it? All things are yours which you have given and which you have done. I am poor and have toiled from my youth and my soul is sometimes saddened to tears, and at times, too, my spirit is disturbed within, for the sufferings which hang over it.

2. I long for the joy of peace, I beseech you for your children's peace, theirs who are fed by you in the light of comfort. If you give peace, if you pour in holy joy, the soul of your servant shall be tuned to song, and devout in your praise. But if you shall have withdrawn yourself, as you are so often wont to do, he will not be able to run the path of your commandments, but rather will his knees sink under him to the beating of his breast, because it is not with him as yesterday and the day before, when your lamp shone above his head, and under the shadow of your wings was he protected from the inrushing temptations.

On Consolation Within 149

3. Just Father, holy and to be forever praised, the hour comes for the testing of your servant. Father, who should be adored, it is fitting that, at this hour, your servant should suffer something for you. Father, ever to be held in reverence, the hour comes, which from eternity you knew beforehand would come, when your servant should in outward show succumb, but, in inward truth live ever in you, for a very little time be held in slight regard, humbled and failing in the eyes of men, wasted by sufferings and weaknesses, so that he should again rise up with you in the dawn of new light and be glorified in heavenly places. Holy Father, so you have appointed, and so you have willed, and that is done which you have yourself commanded.

4. For this is your grace to your friend that he should suffer tribulation in the world, because he loves you, as often as, from whomsoever, and in whatsoever fashion you have permitted it to be done. Without your counsel and providing, and without cause, nothing on earth is done. 'It is good for me, Lord, that you have humbled me, that I may learn your statutes', and that I should cast away all pride of heart and presumptuousness. It is salutary for me that shame has overwhelmed my countenance, that I should seek you for consolation rather than men. I have learned of this, too, to dread your unsearchable judgment, who afflict the just and the impious alike, but not without equity and justice.

5. I thank you that you have not spared my evil deeds, but have lashed me with the blows of love, inflicting sorrows and sending troubles around me and within. There is none to console me of all things under heaven, but you, Lord, my God, the heavenly physician of souls, who strike down and heal, bring down to hell, and bring back again. Your discipline is over me, and your rod itself shall teach me.

6. Look, beloved Father, I am in your hands, and I bow myself beneath the rod of your correction. Smite my back and my neck, that I may bend my crookedness to your will. Make me your dutiful and humble disciple, as you were wont to bless me, that I may walk according to your every nod. I commit myself and all that I have for correction. It is better to be chastised here than in the future. You know all things and everything, and nothing in man's conscience lies hidden from you. Before they are done, you know what things will come to pass; and there is no need for anyone to teach or to advise you about what happens upon earth. You know what aids my advancement, and how much tribulation serves to scrub away the rust of vice. Do your good pleasure on me, for so I do desire, and despise not my sin-filled life, for it is known to no one better and more clearly than to you.

7. Grant me, Lord, to know what I should know, to love that which I should love, to praise that which most pleases you, to value what is precious to you, to detest what is hateful in your sight. Let me not judge according to what the outward eye can see, nor draw conclusions according to what ignorant men can hear, but discern in true judgment concerning visible and spiritual matters, and always in all things seek the will of your goodpleasure.

8. Often, in making judgment, man's senses are deceived; so, too, are the lovers of this world by loving only things which are seen. In what is a man better for being accounted greater by a man? The deceiver deceives the deceiver, the vain the vain, the blind the blind, the weak the weak, when one exalts the other; and when they praise, in their folly, in truth, they more confuse. For, as the humble Saint Francis says: 'As much as each man is in God's eyes, so much he is – no more.'

FIFTY-ONE

On the Need to Pursue Humble Works when we Fall Short of the Greatest

1. 'Son, you are not always strong enough to persevere in a more ardent longing for virtues, nor to continue firmly on a loftier level of contemplation, but sometimes, on account of original sin, you must come down to lower levels, and carry the burden of a corruptible life even against your will and in weariness. As long as you bear a mortal body, you will feel weariness and heaviness of heart. And so, in the flesh, one must often groan over the burden of the flesh, for the reason that you have not the strength to cleave without intermission to spiritual studies and the contemplation of God.'

2. 'And then it is good for you to take refuge in humble works abroad, and refresh yourself with doing good, and to await with strong confidence my coming and visitation from above, to endure your exile and dryness of soul with patience, until again you are visited by me and freed from all anxieties. For I will make you forget your labours and enjoy peace of heart. I will spread wide before you the meadows of the Scriptures, that with wide-open heart you may begin to run the way of my commandments. And you will say: 'The sufferings of this time are not worthy to be compared with the coming glory to be revealed in us.'

152 *The Imitation of Christ*

FIFTY-TWO

On Considering Oneself More Worthy of Chastisement than Comfort

1. Lord, I am not worthy of your consolation, nor of any spiritual visitation; and justly, therefore, do you deal with me when you leave me without resource and desolate. For if I could pour forth tears like the sea, still I should not be worthy of your comfort. Therefore, I am in no way worthy save to be scourged and punished, for often have I grievously offended you and in many ways deeply sinned. Therefore, if true account be taken, I am not worthy of the smallest consolation. But you, gracious and merciful God, because you do not wish your works to perish, to show forth the riches of your goodness towards the vessels of mercy, you design, even beyond his own deserving, to console your servant, beyond all man could do. For your consolations are not like man's discoursings.

2. What have I done, Lord, that you should confer any heavenly consolation on me? I recall that I have done nothing good, but that I have always been disposed to evil, and slow to mend my ways. It is true, and I cannot deny it. If I should say otherwise, you would stand against me, and I should have no defender. What have I deserved for my sins but hell and eternal fire? In truth, I confess that I am worthy of all scorn and contempt, and it is not fitting that I should remain among your worshippers. And although I find this hard to bear, I will, none the less, in truth accuse myself of my sins before you, that the more easily I may deserve to win your mercy.

3. What shall I say, guilty and full of all shame? I have no mouth to utter but this single word: 'I have sinned, Lord, I have sinned'; pity me, pardon me. 'Let me alone for a little, that I may mourn my sorrow, before I go to the land of darkness and the shadow of death.' What do you so much require of a guilty and wretched sinner, save that he be contrite and humble himself for his transgressions? In true contrition, and the heart's humiliation, is born the hope of pardon, the troubled conscience is reconciled, lost grace recovered and a man preserved from the wrath to come, and God and the penitent soul meet each other with a holy kiss.

4. The humble contrition of sinners is acceptable, Lord, to you, a sacrifice more sweetly scented in your sight than the incense of myrrh. This is, too, the pleasant ointment which you wished to be poured on your holy feet, because a contrite and a humbled heart you never have despised. There is the place of refuge from the face of the enemy's wrath. There is made good and washed away whatever defilement has been elsewhere contracted.

FIFTY-THREE

On the Fact that God's Grace is not for the Worldly-minded

1. 'Son, my grace is precious and does not suffer itself to be mixed with alien things nor earthly consolations. You must therefore throw away the hindrances to grace, if you desire to receive its inpouring. Look for a secret place, love to abide there alone, seek comfort from no one, but rather pour out devout prayer to God, that you may keep a contrite mind and a pure conscience. Count the whole world nothing. Set time alone with God before all alien things. For you cannot have free time for me, and equally take delight in things that pass

away. One must be separated from acquaintances and loved ones, and keep the mind away from all temporal comfort. So begs the blessed Apostle Peter, that Christ's faithful bear themselves in this world as strangers and aliens.'

2. 'O, what great confidence shall there be to a man about to die, whom no worldly affection holds back. But a sick soul does not yet understand how to have a heart so set apart from everything, nor does the natural man know the liberty of the spiritual man. And yet, if he truly wishes to be spiritual he must cut himself off from things alike far and near, and beware of no one more than his own self. If you shall have completely overcome yourself, you will easily bring all else into subjection. The perfect victory is to triumph over one's own self. For he who holds his own self in subjection, so that his sensual self obeys reason, and reason in all matters obeys me, he is truly victor over self, and master of the world.'

3. 'If you ardently desire to climb this summit, you must manfully begin and set the axe to the root, so as to tear out and destroy the hidden and extravagant bent towards yourself, and towards all personal and material good. On this vice, man's too extravagant love for his own self, and almost everything which must be conquered at the root depends. This evil conquered truly and subdued, great peace and tranquillity will be unending. But since few strive fully to die completely to themselves, or completely to get free from themselves, they remain in self-entanglement, and cannot in spirit rise above themselves. But he who longs freely to walk with me, must put to death all his base and undisciplined affections, and not cling with desire in selfish love to any thing created.'

FIFTY-FOUR

On the Contrary Workings of Nature and of Grace

1. 'Son, carefully observe the movements of nature and of grace, because they move in quite different directions and with subtlety, and are scarcely to be distinguished save by a spiritual and inwardly enlightened man. All men, indeed, seek good, and profess something good in words and deeds; and so it is that under the guise of good many are deceived.'

2. 'Nature is cunning, and draws away many, ensnares them and deceives, and always has itself for object. Grace walks simply, turns aside from all appearance of evil, and does everything with pure intent for God's sake, in whom ultimately it finds its rest.'

3. 'Nature does not willingly desire to die, to be restricted, or to be in subjection, or, of its own accord, be tamed. But grace is eager to be put to death, resists sensuality, seeks to be subjected, nor desires to exercise personal liberty, loves to be held under discipline, has no desire to lord it over anyone, but to live, to abide, and be always under God, and for God's sake is ready to be subject to any human being.'

4. 'Nature toils for its own advantage, and gives attention to what profit can accrue to it from another, but grace takes thought rather, not of what is useful and advantageous to itself, but what profits many.'

5. 'Nature gladly receives honour and reverence, but grace faithfully ascribes all honour and glory to God.'

6. 'Nature fears shame and contempt, but grace is glad to suffer contumely for Jesus' name.'

7. 'Nature loves leisure and bodily rest, but grace cannot be unoccupied, but gladly embraces toil.'

8. 'Nature seeks to possess things fine and lovely, and turns from what is cheap and crude, but grace delights in the simple and lowly, does not reject the rough, nor shuns being dressed in old clothes.'

9. 'Nature has an eye to temporal things, rejoices in earthly gain, is saddened by loss, is vexed by a small injurious word, but grace looks to eternal things, does not cling to the temporal, is not disturbed by material loss or made angry by harsh words, because it has established its pleasure and its joy in heaven where nothing perishes.'

10. 'Nature is covetous, more gladly receives than gives, and loves what it personally owns, but grace is kind and open-hearted, avoids that which is selfish, is contented with a few things and judges it more blessed to give than to receive.'

11. 'Nature inclines to created things, to the flesh, to vanities and rushing to and fro, but grace draws near to God and the virtues, renounces created things, flees the world, loathes the lusts of the flesh, restricts wanderings abroad, and blushes to appear in public.'

12. 'Nature is glad to hold some outward solace, in which the senses take delight, but grace seeks consolation in God alone, and to find delight in the highest good above all things that are seen.'

13. 'Nature does everything for gain and advantage, and can do nothing freely, but hopes to secure a like return, or better, or praise and favour for benefits conferred, and is eager that its deeds, its gifts and words should be highly valued. Grace, however, looks for nothing temporal, and asks no other reward save God himself for wages; nor desires more of temporal necessities save simply what can serve it in its pursuit of things eternal.'

14. 'Nature rejoices in many friends and kindred, boasts of noble place and high birth, smiles upon the powerful, flatters the rich, and approves those like itself. But grace loves even its enemies, is not exalted by a host of friends, thinks nothing of rank or high birth, save greater virtue be therein, favours rather the poor man than the rich, is at home rather with the guileless than the powerful, rejoices with the truthful, not with the liar, and always urges good men on to strive for better gifts, and to become by virtue like the Son of God.'

15. 'Nature quickly complains of want and trouble, grace constantly endures indigence.'

16. 'Nature bends back everything to itself, and for itself strives and argues, but grace leads all things back to God, whence they flowed at the beginning, ascribes nothing good to itself, nor arrogantly presumes, makes no contention, nor prefers its own opinion to others, but in all feeling and understanding submits itself to eternal wisdom and the examination of God.'

17. 'Nature is eager to know hidden things, and to hear what is new, wishes to make outward show, and to experience many things through the senses, longs to be recognised, and to do those things whence praise and admiration come. But grace does not care to understand the new and curious, because all this has sprung from ancient corruption, and there is nothing new or lasting on the earth. It teaches, therefore, to restrain the senses, to avoid empty complacency and show, humbly to hide what is praiseworthy and admirable, and in everything, and in all knowledge, to seek the fruit of usefulness and God's praise and honour. It has no desire for itself or what it has to be proclaimed, but longs that God be blessed in his gifts, he who bestows all things out of pure love.'

18. This grace is a supernatural light and a kind of special gift of God, and peculiarly a small mark of the chosen ones, and an earnest of eternal salvation, which lifts a man above earthly things to the heavenly things which he should love and makes the carnal spiritual. In proportion, therefore as nature is suppressed and conquered, so much is greater grace poured in, and day by day the inner man, by fresh visitations is reshaped according to the image of God.

FIFTY-FIVE

On Nature's Corruption and the Efficacy of God's Grace

1. Lord, my God, who made me in your own image and likeness, grant me that grace which you have shown to be so great and vital for salvation, that I may overcome my most evil nature, which drags me to sin and to perdition. For I feel in my flesh the law of sin, contradicting the law of my mind, and in many things leading me captive to obey my sensual nature; nor can I resist its passions, unless your most holy grace, poured hot into my heart, aid me.

2. Your grace is needed, and great grace, too, to conquer nature, ever prone to evil from its youth up. For, fallen through the

first man, Adam, and corrupted through sin, the punishment of this stain fell upon all men, so that nature itself, though established good and straight by you, since its urges, left to itself, drag towards evil and lower things, is now synonymous with vice and the weakness of nature's corruption. For the small strength which remains is like some spark hidden in ashes. This is natural reason, enveloped in thick darkness, still possessing a discernment of good and evil, and a distinction between the true and the false, though impotent to fulfil all that it approves, and not yet in possession of truth's full light, and healthiness in all it feels.

3. This is why, my God, though 'I delight in your law according to the inner man', knowing that your commandment will be good, just and holy, reproving, too, all evil, and the sin which must be shunned, 'with the flesh I serve the law of sin', in obeying rather sensuality than reason. Hence it comes about that 'though to will good is present with me, I find not how to perform it'. Hence I often purpose many good things, but because grace is not present to aid my weakness, I recoil before light resistance, and fail. Hence it happens that I recognise the way of perfection, and how I ought to act I see clearly enough, but bowed beneath the weight of my own corruption, I do not rise to more perfect things.

4. O, how supremely necessary to me, Lord, is your grace to begin any good thing, to promote it and perfect it! For without, it I can do nothing, but I can do all things in you if your grace makes me strong. O, true heavenly grace, without which our own merits are nothing, and none of nature's gifts weigh anything. Arts, riches, beauty, bravery, wits or eloquence are worth nothing with you, Lord, without grace. For the gifts of nature are common to good and bad, but the special gift

of the chosen is grace or love, with which endowed they are counted worthy of eternal life. So superlative is this grace, that neither the gift of prophecy, nor the working of miracles, nor any manner of lofty speculation is considered anything without it. But neither faith, nor hope, nor other virtues are acceptable to you without love and grace.

5. O, most blessed grace which makes the poor in spirit rich in virtues, and renders him who is rich in many things humble in spirit. Come, descend to me, fill me in the morning with your comfort, lest my soul faint for weariness and dryness of mind. I beg, Lord, that I may find grace in your eyes, for your grace is sufficient for me, even when I win not those other things for which nature longs. Ever tempted and harassed with many tribulations, I will fear no evil while your grace is with me. It is itself my strength, my counsel and my help. It is more powerful than all enemies, more wise than all the wise.

6. It is the mistress of truth, the teacher of discipline, the light of the heart, the solace of anxiety, the banisher of sorrow, the deliverer from fear, the nurse of devotion, and the prompter of tears. What am I without it, but dry wood and a useless stump to be uprooted? Let your grace towards me, Lord, go before and follow behind, and make me continually eager for good works through Jesus Christ your Son. Amen.

FIFTY-SIX

On the Obligation of Self-denial and Imitating Christ by Way of the Cross

1. 'Son, just as far as you can get out of yourself, so far you will be able to pass into me. Just as it brings inward peace to

covet no outward thing, so to forsake self inwardly, joins one to God. I want you to learn complete self-abnegation in my will, without answering back or complaint. Follow me – I am the way, the truth, and the life. There is no journeying without a way, no knowing without truth, no living without life. I am the way which you must follow, the truth you must believe, the life for which you must hope. I am the way imperishable, the truth infallible, the life everlasting. I am the straightest way, the highest truth, the true life, the blessed life, the life uncreated. If you remain in my way you will know the truth, the truth will make you free, and you will lay hold of eternal life.'

2. 'If you wish to enter into eternal life keep the commandments. If you wish to know the truth, believe me. If you wish to be perfect, sell everything. If you wish to be my disciple renounce your very self. If you wish to possess the blessed life, despise the present life. If you wish to be exalted in heaven, humiliate yourself on earth. If you wish to reign with me, carry your cross with me. For only the servants of the cross will find the way of blessedness and true life.'

3. Lord Jesus, since your way is narrow, and despised by the world, grant me to imitate you in despising the world. For the servant is not greater than his lord, nor the disciple above his master. Let your servant be occupied with your life because there lies my salvation and true holiness. Whatever I read or hear outside of it, does not refresh me, nor fully delight me.

4. 'Son, because you know these matters and have read them all, blessed are you if you shall do them. He who has my commandments and keeps them, he it is who loves me, and I

will love him and reveal myself to him, and I will make him sit with me in my Father's kingdom.'

5. Lord Jesus, just as you have said and promised, even so let it come about, and let it fall to me to be deserving. I have taken up, taken up from your hand the cross. I will carry it, and I will carry it to death, as you have laid it on me. Truly, the life of a good monk is the cross, but it is the guide to paradise. A beginning has been made; it is not permitted to go back, and it must not be abandoned.

6. Come, brothers, let us march on, Jesus will be with us. For Jesus' sake we took up this cross. For Jesus' sake let us go on bearing it. He will be our helper, who is our leader, and the one who went before. Look, our king strides on ahead of us, and he will fight for us. Let us follow manfully, nor fear those things which terrify; let us be prepared to die bravely in battle, and let us not bring reproach against our honour by flying from the cross.

FIFTY-SEVEN

On not Despairing too Greatly in Failures

1. 'Son, endurance and humility in adversity please me more than much consolation and devotion in prosperity. Why does a small thing said against you sadden you? If it had been more, you should not have been disturbed. But now let it pass; it is not the first, not new, nor will it be the last, if you live long enough. You are manly enough so long as no adversity comes your way. You give good advice, too, and know how to strengthen others by your words, but when sudden trouble comes to your own door, you are wanting in advice and strength. Look to your own frailty, which you quite often experience in trifling affairs; yet these things happen, when they and their like befall you, for your salvation.'

2. 'Put it from your heart, as best you know how to do; and if trouble has touched you, still do not let it cast you down, or tangle you for long. At least endure patiently, if you cannot gladly. Although you are reluctant to hear it, and feel angry, hold yourself in, nor suffer anything extravagant to pass your lips, by which little ones may be caused to stumble. The disturbance stirred will soon be stilled, and grief of heart will be sweetened with grace returning. I am still alive, says the Lord, prepared to help you, and to give consolation beyond that which you know, if you will trust in me and devoutly call upon me.'

3. 'Be more calm of spirit, and gird yourself for greater endurance. All is not made useless, if you find yourself quite often afflicted or grievously tempted. You are a man, and not God, flesh, not an Angel. How could you always remain in the same state of virtue, when an Angel in heaven fell, and the first man in paradise. I am he who lifts up those that mourn to safety, and promotes those who recognise their weakness to my own divinity.'

4. Lord, blessed be your word, sweet to my mouth beyond honey and the honeycomb. What should I do in my tribulations and troubles so great, if you were not to comfort me with your holy discourses? Provided at length I reach the haven of salvation, why should I care what sufferings I endure? Grant a good ending, a happy passing from this world. Remember me, my God, and lead me by a straight way to your kingdom.   Amen.

FIFTY-EIGHT

On not Searching into Higher Matters and God's Hidden Judgments

1. 'Son, beware of disputing high matters and the hidden judgments of God: why this man is so passed over and that one taken up into favour so great; why, too, this one is so afflicted, and that one so exceedingly exalted. These things go beyond human understanding, nor has any reasoning or argument strength to look into God's judgment. When, therefore, the enemy makes these suggestions to you, or even when some inquisitive men make enquiry, reply with that saying of the Prophet: Just, you are, Lord, and your judgment straight. Or this: The Lord's judgments are true and justified in their own right. My judgments are to be feared, not discussed, because they are beyond the understanding of the mind of man.'

2. 'Do not, furthermore, inquire or argue about the merits of the Saints, who is more saintly than another or greater in the kingdom of the heavens. Such things often beget useless quarrels and arguments, and also feed pride and empty glory, whence arise envies and dissensions, as one man arrogantly prefers this Saint, that another. To wish to know and explore such matters produces no fruit, but rather displeases the Saints, because I am not the God of dissension but of peace, and peace consists more in true humility than in self-exaltation.

3. Some are drawn by zeal of love to these Saints or with fuller affection to those, but affection human rather than divine. It is I who established all the Saints; I gave them grace; I endowed them with glory. I know the merits of each of them. I went before them with the blessings of my sweetness. I foreknew my loved ones from everlasting; I chose them out of the world, they did not choose me. I called them through grace, I drew them through mercy; I led them through various temptations. I poured on them wondrous consolations, I gave them perseverance and crowned their endurance.'

4. 'I know the first and the last, I embrace them all with love inestimable. I am to be praised among all my Saints; I am to be blessed above all things, and honoured in each one whom I have so gloriously exalted and predestined, with no antecedent merits of their own. He, therefore, who despises the least of my own, does not honour the great, for I made both small and great. And he who detracts from any one of the Saints, detracts also from me and all others in the kingdom of the heavens. All are one through the bond of love, thinking, wishing the same thing and all love each other in unity.'

5. 'But as yet – something much loftier – they love me more than themselves and their merits. For, caught up above themselves, and drawn beyond self-love, they move on wholly into love of me, in whom, too, they find delightsome rest. There is nothing which can turn them aside or press them down, for they are full of everlasting truth, and burn with the fire of inextinguishable love. Let, therefore, carnal and natural men, who know nothing beyond their own selfish joys, hold their peace, and not discuss the state of the Saints. They take away and add according to their whim, not as it pleases eternal truth.'

6. 'In many it is ignorance, especially of those who, with small enlightenment, rarely know what it is to love anyone with perfect spiritual love. They are still much drawn by natural affection and human friendship to these folk or those, and

just as, on a lower plane, they think about themselves, so they imagine things heavenly to be. But there is distance beyond compare between what faulty men think, and those things which the enlightened explore by heaven's revelation.'

7. 'Beware, therefore, son, lest you handle inquisitively those matters which surpass your knowledge, but make this rather your care and purpose, that you may be found, though the very least, in the kingdom of God. And if one should know who is holier than another, or who may be held greater in the kingdom of the heavens, what good would this knowledge do him, unless through this understanding he should humiliate himself before me, and rise to greater praise of my name? He acts far more acceptably to God, who thinks of the enormity of his sins, and the insignificance of his virtues, and how far he falls short of the perfection of the Saints, than he who argues about who is great, who small among them. It is better to plead with the Saints with devout prayers and tears, and with humble mind to implore their glorious support, than with empty curiosity to pry into their secrets.'

8. 'They are right well contented, if men know how to be content and to control their empty talk. They do not glory in their own merits, for they ascribe no goodness to themselves, but all to me, because I have given all things to them from my boundless love. With such love of the Godhead and overwhelming joy are they filled, that nought of glory is wanting to them, and nothing of happiness can fail. All the Saints, the higher they are in glory, the more lowly they are in themselves, and live nearer to me, and dearer. That is why you have it written that they cast their crowns before God, and fell upon their faces in the presence of the Lamb, and worshipped him who lives for ever and ever.'

9. 'Many inquire who is greatest in the kingdom of God, who do not know whether they will be worthy of being numbered among the least. It is great to be even the least in heaven, where all are great, because all will be called, as they will actually be, the sons of God. The least shall be as a thousand, and the sinner of a hundred years shall die. For when the disciples asked who is greater in the kingdom of the heavens, thus did they hear in reply: Unless you be converted and become as little children, you will not enter into the kingdom of the heavens. Whoever therefore shall humiliate himself like this little one, he is the greater in the kingdom of the heavens.'

10. 'Alas for those who disdain to humble themselves willingly like little children, for the gate of the heavenly kingdom is low, and will now allow them to enter. Alas for the rich who have their consolation here, for when the poor are entering the kingdom of God, they shall stand outside lamenting. Rejoice you humble, and exult you poor, for yours is the kingdom of God if only you walk in truth.'

FIFTY-NINE

On the need to Fix all Hope and Confidence in God

1. Lord, what is my confidence, which I have in this life, or what greater solace have I from all that can be seen under heaven? Is it not you, Lord my God, whose mercy is beyond numbering? Where has it been well with me without you? Or where could it be ill with you beside me? I prefer to be poor for your sake, than rich without you. I choose rather with you to be a pilgrim on the earth, than without you to possess heaven. Where you are, there is heaven; and there is death and hell, where you are not. You fill my longing; and so I must sigh, cry out and earnestly pray for you. In a word I can trust fully in nothing, but in you alone my God. You are my hope, my confidence and my most trusty comforter in everything.

2. All seek those things which are their own, you set before me my salvation and my progress alone, and turn everything to good for me. Even though you expose me to various temptations and adversities, you direct it all to my advantage, for it has been your wont to test your loved ones in a thousand ways. And in such testing you should be no less loved and praised than if you should fill me with heaven's consolations.

3. In you, therefore, Lord God, I place my whole hope and refuge, on you I place all my tribulation and anguish, for whatever I observe apart from you, I find to be wholly weak and unstable. For many friends will be of no avail, nor will strong allies be able to aid, nor wise counsellors to give a useful answer, nor the books of learned men console, nor any precious object ransom, nor secret place conceal, if you yourself do not stand by to aid, to help, strengthen, console, instruct and guard.

4. For all things which seem to make for peace and happiness are nothing, if you are not there, and in truth confer no happiness. For you are the fountain of all good, the height of life, and the depth of all fine speech, and in you above all things to hope, is your servants' strongest consolation. On you are my eyes, in you I trust, my God, Father of mercies..Bless and sanctify my soul with heavenly blessing, that it may become your sacred dwelling-place, the seat of your eternal glory, and that nothing may be found in the temple of your divinity,

which could offend the eyes of your majesty. According to the greatness of your goodness, and the multitude of your mercies, look upon me and hear the prayers of your poor servant, a far exile in the kingdom of the shadow of death. Protect and preserve the soul of your poor servant amid the many perils of a corruptible life, and, your grace accompanying, direct him along the path of peace to the fatherland of everlasting light.

BOOK FOUR

On the Sacrament of the Altar

On the Deep Reverence with which Christ must be Received

The Voice of Christ

'Come to me all who labour and are heavy-laden and I will refresh you,' says the Lord. 'The bread which I shall give is my flesh, for the life of the world. Take it and eat, this is my Body, which is surrendered for you. Do this in memory of me. He who eats my flesh and drinks my blood, abides in me and I in him. The words which I have spoken to you are spirit and life.'

The Voice of the Disciple

1. These are your words, Christ, eternal Truth, although not said at one time, nor written together in one place. Therefore, because they are your words and true, all of them must be received by me with gratitude and trust. They are your words and you have said them; they are also my words because you have uttered them for my salvation. Gladly I receive them from your mouth, that they may be more firmly planted in my heart. Words of such great trustiness, full of sweetness and love, stir me, but my own sins terrify me, and my impure conscience beats me back from receiving mysteries so

great. The sweetness of your words beckons me on, but the multitude of my sins weighs me down.

2. You bid me to approach you with confidence, if I wish to have a part in you, and that I may receive the nourishment of immortality, if I desire to win eternal life and glory. 'Come,' you say, 'all you who labour and are heavy-laden, and I will refresh you.' O, sweet and friendly word in a sinner's ear, that you, Lord God, invite the needy and the poor to the communion of your most holy Body! Who am I, Lord, that I should presume to approach you? Look, the heaven of heavens does not contain you, and you say: 'Come to me, all of you.'

3. What does it mean, that most holy condescension, and so friendly an invitation? In what way shall I make bold to come, who am conscious of nothing good in myself on which I can presume? In what way shall I bring you into my house, who have so often affronted your most kindly face? Angels and Archangels stand in awe of you, the saintly, and the just fear you, and you say: 'Come to me, all of you.' Unless it were you, Lord, who said this, who would believe it to be true? And unless it were your command, who would attempt to draw near?

4. Look, Noah, a just man, laboured for a hundred years building the ark, that with a few he might be saved. And how shall I, in one hour, be able to prepare myself to take up with reverence the builder of the world? Moses, your great servant and special friend, made an ark of imperishable wood, which he covered over with the purest gold, that he might store in it the tablets of the law. And I, a loathsome creature, shall I dare to take up lightly the founder of the law, and the maker of life? Solomon, the wisest of Israel's kings, built, in seven years, a magnificent temple in praise of your name, and for eight days celebrated the ceremony of its dedication, offered a thousand peace-offerings, and, with trumpet-blast and jubilation, brought the ark of covenant, with solemnity, into the place prepared for it. And I, unhappy one and poorest of men, how shall I bring you into my house, I who scarce know how to spend a half-hour devoutly? And would that I spent once, even one half-hour worthily!

5. O, my God, how much they strove to please you! Alas, how trifling is what I do! What a short time I spend when I am preparing myself for Communion! Rarely am I quite composed, most rarely cleansed of all distraction. And surely in the saving presence of your Godhead, no unbecoming thought should arise, nor any created thing lay hold upon me, for it is not an Angel, but the Lord of Angels, whom I am about to receive as my guest.

6. And yet there is a vast difference between the ark of the covenant with its relics, and your most pure Body with its unspeakable virtues, between those sacrifices of the law which showed in symbol that which was to be, and the true sacrifice of your Body, the consummation of all the ancient sacrifices.

7. Why then am I not more on fire before your awesome presence? Why do I not prepare myself with greater care to take up your holy things, when those holy Patriarchs and Prophets of old, kings, too, and princes with the whole people, showed such heartfelt devotion towards the divine service?

8. The most devout King David danced before the ark of God with all his strength, remembering the benefits granted of old to his ancestors; he made musical instruments of varied sorts, and composed psalms, and appointed them to be sung with joy, and did so himself often with the harp, inspired with the Holy Spirit's grace; he taught the people of Israel to praise God

with the whole heart, and with one voice of harmony each day to praise and to extol him. If such devotion then was exercised, and such memorial of God's praise was manifest before the ark of witness, how great now, by me and all Christ's people, should reverence and devotion be shown in the presence of the Sacrament, and in taking up the most precious Body of Christ?

9. Many rush to different places to visit the relics of the Saints, and wonder to hear the deeds they did; they look on the vast buildings of their shrines, and kiss their bones enwrapped in silks and gold. And look, you are here, beside me on the altar, my God, Saint of Saints, Creator of men, and Lord of Angels. Often in seeing such things, it is the curiosity of men, and the novelty of what they look upon, and small fruit of better living which is carried home, especially where there is much frivolous rushing about without real repentance. But here, in the Sacrament of the altar, you are wholly present, my God, the man Christ Jesus, where also the abundant fruit of eternal salvation is fully received, as often as it is taken up worthily and devoutly. But any levity, curiosity or sensuality does not bring one to this, but strong faith, devout hope and sincere love.

10. O God, unseen creator of the world, how wondrously you deal with us, how sweetly and graciously you arrange for your chosen ones, to whom you offer your own self for them to receive in the Sacrament! For this surpasses all reach of thought, this chiefly draws the heart of the devout and fires their love. For even your true faithful ones who order their whole life for betterment, often receive from this most worthy Sacrament great grace of devotion, and love of virtue.

11. O, admirable and hidden grace of the Sacrament, which only Christ's faithful know, but which the faithless and the

servants of sin cannot experience! In this Sacrament spiritual grace is conferred, and lost virtue made good in the soul, and beauty marred by sin returns. This grace is sometimes so great that, out of the fulness of devotion that it gives, even the feeble body feels ampler powers bestowed upon it.

12. It must nevertheless be a matter for grief and great pity that, lukewarm and negligent, we are not drawn with deeper feeling to receive Christ, in whom stands the whole hope and merit of those who must be saved, for he is our sanctification and our redemption, the consolation of wayfarers, and the eternal fruitfulness of the Saints. And so it is truly a matter for grief, that many attend so little to this healthgiving mystery, which makes heaven glad, and preserves the whole wide world. Alas, the blindness and hardness of the human heart, not to attend the more to this gift so unutterable, and from daily custom to slide away to carelessness.

13. For if this most holy Sacrament should be celebrated in one place only, and consecrated by one priest only in the world, with what greater desire do you think would men be affected towards that place, and such a priest of God, so that they might see the divine mysteries celebrated? But now many are made priests, and Christ is offered up in many places, so that the grace and love of God towards man should appear so much the greater, as the Holy Communion is more widely spread through all the world. Thanks to you, good Jesus, eternal pastor, who deigned to refresh us poor exiles with your precious Body and Blood, and even with the speech of our own mouth to invite us to partake of these mysteries, saying: 'Come to me all you who labour and are heavy laden, and I will refresh you.'

On the Great Goodness and Love of God Shown in the Sacrament

The Voice of the Disciple

1. Trusting in your goodness and great mercy, Lord, I draw near sick to the Saviour, hungry and thirsty to the fountain of life, needy to the King of heaven, a servant to the Master, a creature to the Creator, desolate to my trusty Comforter. But whence this boon, that you should come to me? Who am I that you should offer me yourself? How dares the sinner appear in your presence? And you, how do you deign to come to the sinner? You know your servant, and you know that he has nothing good in himself, that you should bestow this upon him. I confess, therefore, my worthlessness, I acknowledge your goodness, I praise your trusty tenderness, I give thanks for your exceeding love. You do this for your own Sake, not for my merits, that your goodness might be made more known to me, your love more abundantly outpoured, your lowliness more perfectly commended. Since, then, this is your pleasure, and you have bade it so be done, your condescension also pleases me, and may my iniquity not stand in its way.

2. O, sweetest and most kindly Jesus, what great reverence and giving of thanks, along with endless praise, is due to you for the taking in our hands of your holy Body, whose dignity no man is found able to express. But what shall I think about in this Communion, in approaching my Lord, whom I am unable to revere as I ought, and whom yet I long to take into my hands with devotion? On what can I better and more wholesomely think, than of humiliating myself utterly before you, and setting your boundless goodness above me? I praise you, my God and exalt you for ever. I praise you, my God and cast myself down for you into the depth of my worthlessness.

3. Look, you are the Saint of Saints, and I am the dregs of sinners. Look, you stoop to me, who am not worthy to look on you. Look, you come to me, you wish to be with me, you invite me to be your guest. You are willing to give me heavenly food and the bread of Angels to eat, no other forsooth, than you yourself, the living bread, you who came down from heaven to give life to the world.

4. Look, whence love comes, what manner of condescension illumines it! What great giving of thanks and praises are due to you for these things! O, how wholesome and profitable was your plan, when you set it up! How sweet and pleasant the banquet, when you gave yourself for food! O, how wondrous is your working, Lord, how mighty your strength, how infallible your truth! For you uttered the word, and all things were made; and this was done, which you commanded.

5. Wondrous it is, and worthy of faith, transcending the intelligence of man, that you, Lord, my God, truly God and man, are contained entire under the common appearance of bread divine, and are eaten by the one who takes it, without being consumed. You, Lord of the universe, who have no need of anyone, willed, through your Sacrament, to live in us, keep my heart and my body undefiled, that, with joyous and pure conscience, I may be fit more often to celebrate the mysteries, and receive, for my eternal salvation, those things which you have consecrated and instituted, chiefly for your own glory and a memorial everlasting.

6. Rejoice, my soul, and thank God for a gift so noble and for unique consolation left for you in this vale of tears. For as often as you practise this mystery again and receive the Body of Christ, so often do you perform the work of your redemption, and are made to share all the merits of Christ. For the love of Christ never knows diminution, and the greatness of his atonement is never exhausted. And so always, with fresh renewal of your mind, you should prepare yourself for this, and with attentive meditation weigh the great mystery of salvation. As great, new, joyous should it appear to you when you celebrate or hear the service of Communion, as if, on that same day, Christ first descending to the Virgin's womb, had been made a man, or, hanging on the cross, should be suffering and dying for man's salvation.

THREE

On the Value of Frequent Communion

The Voice of the Disciple

1. Look, I come to you, Lord, that it might be well with me through your gift, and that I may rejoice at your holy banquet, which you have made ready, in your sweetness, for the poor. Look, all is in you, which I can and should desire; you are my salvation and redemption, hope and strength, honour and glory. Make glad, therefore, today the soul of your servant, because to you, Lord Jesus, I have lifted up my soul. I long, at this moment, devoutly and reverently to receive you; I desire to bring you into my home, so that with Zacchaeus I may be made worthy to be blessed by you, and numbered among 'Abraham's children'. My soul eagerly desires your Body, and my heart longs to be united with you.

2. Give yourself to me, and it suffices, for apart from you no solace is availing. Without you, I cannot exist, and without your visitation, I have not strength to live. And so I must often come to you, and receive you once more, as the medicine of my salvation, lest I faint on the way, deprived of heaven's nourishment. For it was thus that you, most merciful Jesus, preaching to the multitudes and healing various diseases, once said: 'I do not want to send them home hungry, in case they grow faint on the way.' Do, therefore, thus with me, for you left yourself, for the consolation of the faithful, in the Sacrament. For you are the sweet refreshment of the soul, and he who has fed upon you worthily, will be partaker and heir of eternal glory. Essential is it, indeed, for me, who so often slip and sin, so quickly grow cold and faint, to refresh, cleanse and fire myself through frequent prayers, confessions, and the holy receiving of your body – lest by abstinence too long, I may fall away from my holy purpose.

3. For bent are the feelings of man to evil from his youth, and unless you help with medicine divine, man soon slips to greater evil. Therefore Holy Communion draws one back from ill, and makes one strong in good. For if now I am so careless and so cool, when I take part in the service, what would happen if I did not take the remedy, and did not seek a help so great? And though every day I am not fit or prepared in mind to participate, I shall, none the less, give heed at proper times to receive the divine mysteries, and to make myself partaker in grace so great. For this is the one chief consolation of the faithful soul, so long as it is a pilgrim and absent from you in a mortal body, often, with a mind devout, to receive him whom it loves.

4. O, wondrous condescension of your trusty love around us, that you, Lord God, creator and life-giver of all spirits, should deign to come to a soul utterly weak, and with your whole Godhead and humanity feed full its hungering. O, happy mind and blessed soul, who is counted worthy to receive you, Lord God, devoutly, and, in receiving, be filled again with

spiritual joy! O, what a great God it receives, what a loved guest it takes in, how delightful a companion it welcomes, how beautiful and noble a husband does it embrace, beyond all other beloved ones, and to be adored beyond all things longed for! Let them be silent before your face, my most sweet beloved one, sky and earth and all that which adorns them, because whatever praise or glory they have, is because you condescended freely to bestow it, nor will they attain to the glory of your name, whose wisdom is beyond all measuring.

FOUR

On the Many Blessings Bestowed on the Devout Communicant

The Voice of the Disciple

1. Lord, my God, go ahead of your servant with the blessings of your sweetness, that I may prove fit to approach worthily and devoutly your most glorious Sacrament. Awaken my heart to yourself, and strip me of my heavy slothfulness. Visit me with your healthgiving, that in spirit I may taste your sweetness, the sweetness which, in this Sacrament, lies as if in a brimming spring. Lighten, too, my eyes that I may look upon so great a mystery, and strengthen me that I may believe it with a faith that has no doubt. For it is your working, not the might of man, your holy institution, not man's devising. For no one is found fit in himself to grasp and understand these things, for they are above even the keen wisdom of the Angels. What, therefore, shall I be able to search into and grasp of a secret so high and holy, I who am an unworthy sinner, earth and ashes?

2. Lord, in my heart's simplicity, in good, strong faith and in accordance with your will, I come to you with hope and reverence,

and truly believe that you are present here in the Sacrament, God and man. It is, therefore, your will that I receive you, and make myself one with you in love. And so I pray for your mercy, and beg that special grace be given me to this end that I may totally be lost in you, and suffused with love, and no more admit into myself any other consolation. For this most lofty and glorious Sacrament is salvation of soul and body, the medicine for all sickness of the spirit, in which my sins are healed, passions bridled, temptations conquered and diminished, greater grace poured in, virtue, once begun, increased, faith made more firm, hope made more robust, and love fired and spread abroad.

3. For, indeed, in the Sacrament you have bestowed many blessings, and still, again and again, bestow them on your loved ones, who devoutly communicate, my God, uplifter of my soul, repairer of man's infirmity, and giver of all the heart's consolation. For you pour into them much consolation against all manner of tribulations, and from the depths of their own misery lift them to the hope of your protection, and with some new grace refresh and enlighten them, so that those who, before Communion, first had been conscious of anxiety and lovelessness, afterwards, refreshed with heaven's food and drink, discover themselves changed for the better. It is for this reason you with purpose deal with your chosen ones, that they may truly acknowledge, and clearly experience what measure of infirmity they have in themselves, and what goodness and grace they acquire from you – for of themselves they are cold, hard and without devotion, but by you they are made worthy to be warm, eager and devout. For who in humility approaches the spring of sweetness, and does not bring a little sweetness back from it? Or who, standing by an ample fire, does not perceive a little warmth from it? And you are a fountain ever full and flowing over, a fire continually burning and never dying down.

4. So, if I am not permitted to drink deep from the fulness of the spring, until I thirst no more, I shall still place my mouth to the outlet of this heavenly channel, so that at least I may take a tiny drop from it to quench my thirst, and not dry up deep within. And if I cannot be yet wholly of heaven, and fired as the Cherubim and Seraphim are fired, I shall still try to follow up devotion, and prepare my heart to catch a small flame from the divine fire from the reception of the life-giving Sacrament. But whatever is wanting to me, good Jesus, most holy Saviour, do you supply me of your kindliness and grace, who have deigned to call all to you, saying: 'Come to me all who labour and are heavy-laden and I will refresh you.'

5. I labour, indeed, by the sweat of my face, I am tortured by the heart's sorrow, I am burdened by sins, I am disquieted by temptations, I am tangled and loaded by many evil passions, and there is no one to help me, set me free, and save me, except you, Lord God, my Saviour, to whom I commit myself and all I have, that you may keep me and lead me through to life eternal. Receive me for the praise and glory of your name, you have prepared your Body and your Blood to be my food and drink. Grant, Lord God of my Salvation, that by my oft-coming to your mystery, the zeal of my devotion may grow.

FIVE

On the Dignity of the Sacrament and the Priestly Office

The Voice of the Beloved

1. 'If you should have the purity of an Angel, and the holiness of the holy John the Baptiser, you would not be worthy to receive or to administer this Sacrament. For it is not due to the merits of men that a man should consecrate and administer the Sacrament of Christ, and take for food the bread of Angels. It is a vast mystery, and mighty dignity of Priests, that to them is given what is not allowed the Angels. For Priests alone, properly ordained in the Church, have the power of celebrating and consecrating the Body of Christ. For, indeed, a Priest is a servant of God, using the word of God by God's command and institution. But God is there, chief author and invisible executor, to whom is subject all that he has willed, and everything obeys what he has ordered.'

2. 'You ought, therefore, the more to believe God omnipotent in this most excellent Sacrament, than your own understanding or any visible symbol. Therefore with fear and reverence must this work be approached. Look to yourself, and see whose service it is that was committed to you by the laying on of the Bishop's hands. Look, you were made a Priest and consecrated for the celebration. Take care now that, faithfully and devoutly, at its proper time, you offer the sacrifice of God, and show yourself blameless. You have not lightened your burden, but are now bound with a tighter chain of discipline, and pledged to a higher level of holiness. A Priest should be adorned with all the virtues. His mode of life must be, not with the popular and common ways of men, but with the Angels in heaven and saintly men on earth.'

3. 'A Priest, wearing his holy vestments, stands in the place of Christ to pray to God with supplication and humility for himself and all the people. He has, before him and behind the sign of the Lord's cross, to bring to remembrance continually the passion of Christ. Before him he bears the cross of Christ on his chasuble, so that he may diligently trace out Christ's footsteps, and be zealous fervently to follow them. Behind him he is signed with the cross, that he may meekly bear for God all manner of trials brought on him by others. Before him he bears the cross, that he may grieve for his own sins, and behind that, in compassion, he may weep for sins committed by others, and know that he has been placed midway between God and the sinner, and not grow cold in prayer and holy offering, until he prevail to win grace and mercy. Whenever a Priest ministers, he honours God, makes the Angels glad, aids the living, wins rest for the dead, and makes himself partaker of all good.'

On Preparing for Communion

The Voice of the Disciple

1. When I consider your majesty, Lord, and my own baseness, I tremble exceedingly and am abashed within myself. For if I do not draw near, I run away from life; and if I shall intrude unworthily, I incur displeasure. What therefore shall I do, my God, my helper and counsellor, in dire needs?

2. Do you teach me the straight way; set before me some brief exercise, befitting Holy Communion. For it is profitable, doubtless, to know in what fashion I should with devotion and reverence make my heart ready for you, to receive wholesomely your Sacrament, or even to celebrate so great and divine a mystery.

SEVEN

On Self-examination and Resolution for Amendment

The Voice of the Beloved

1. 'Above all things, with deep humility of heart and prayerful reverence, with full faith and earnest desire to honour God,

the Priest of God must approach the celebration, the handling and the receiving of this Sacrament. Carefully examine your conscience, and, as far as in you lies, cleanse and clarify it with true penitence and humble confession, so that you have no burden, nor know of any which might bring remorse, or hinder free access. Hold in displeasure all your sins in general, and more in particular grieve and mourn for your transgressions of each and every day. And if time allows, in the secret place of your heart, confess to God all the miseries of your passions.'

2. 'Sigh and grieve that you are still so carnal and worldly, still so unable to count your passions dead, so full of the movements of desire, so unguarded in your senses' outreach, so tangled often by a host of unprofitable imaginings, so much bent to things outside yourself, so careless of what lies within, so prone to laughter and frivolity, so hardened against weeping and the thrust of conscience, so ready for easier ways and that which pleases the flesh, so sluggish in austerity and zeal, so inquisitive to hear the news and look on lovely things, so loth to lay hold of the humble and despised, so greedy to possess much, so sparing in giving, so grasping to retain, so thoughtless in speaking and so uncontrolled in keeping silence, so disordered in your manners, and pushing in action, so eager over food, so deaf to God's word, so quick to rest, so slow to work, so awake for gossip, so sleepy in holy vigils, so hasty to finish, so wandering in attention, so careless in your hourly devotions, so cold in celebration, so dry in communicating, so quickly distracted, so slow in fully regaining self-control, so swiftly moved to wrath, so apt to be displeased with another, so given to judging, so stern in reproof, so glad when all goes well, so weak in adversity, so often making good resolutions, and carrying little into effect.'

3. 'When these and your other failings have been confessed and grieved over, with sorrow and displeasure at your own weakness, establish a strong resolution always to amend your life, and move on to the better. Then with full resignation and entire will, offer yourself for the honour of my name on the altar of your heart, a full and perpetual sacrifice, by committing, in a word, your body and your soul faithfully to me, so that thus you may be reckoned worthy to draw near and offer sacrifice to God, and to take up wholesomely the Sacrament of my Body.'

4. 'For there is no worthier sacrifice, no satisfaction greater for the washing away of sins, than to offer up one's own self to God, purely and entirely, with the offering of Christ's Body in the Celebration of Communion. If a man shall have so done, as far as in him lies, and have truly repented, as often as he shall come to me for pardon and for grace: "I live", says the Lord to him, "I who do not desire the death of the sinner, but rather that he may be converted and live, for I shall no more remember his sins, but all shall be forgiven him." '

EIGHT

On the Offering of Christ on the Cross and Self-resignation

The Voice of the Beloved

1. 'Just as I, of my own will, offered myself to God the Father for your sins upon the cross, with outstretched arms and naked body, so that nothing remained in me that was not wholly transformed into a sacrifice of divine atonement, so you, too, as much as you avail in heart, must offer your own self to me, of your free will, for an offering pure and holy, daily at Communion, with all your strength and love. What more do I require of you than that you strive to resign yourself completely to me? I care nothing for what you give apart from yourself, for I seek not your gift, but you.'

2. 'Just as it would not be enough for you if you had all things but not me, so it will not be possible to please me, whatever you have given, apart from offering yourself. Offer up yourself to me, and give yourself wholly for God, and your offering will be accepted. Look, I offered myself wholly to the Father for you; I also gave my whole Body and Blood for you for food, that I might be wholly yours, and you should remain mine. But if you stand upon yourself, and do not offer yourself freely to my will, the offering is not fully made, nor will union between us be complete. Therefore, the willing offering of your own self into the hands of God, must go before everything you do, if you wish to attain liberty and grace. For this is why so few are enlightened and made free within, because they do not know how to deny themselves completely. My statement stands: "Unless a man renounces all that he possesses he cannot be my disciple." Therefore, if you desire to be my disciple, offer yourself to me with all your affections.'

NINE

On the Need to Offer Self and all we have to God and Pray for all Men

The Voice of the Disciple

1. Lord, all things are yours in heaven and on earth. I long to offer myself to you for a freewill offering, and to remain forever yours. Lord, in the sincerity of my heart, I offer myself to you today to serve forever, for obedience and for a sacrifice of unending praise. Receive me with this holy offering of your precious Body, which today I offer you, in the presence of Angels, invisibly around, that it may be for salvation for me and for all the people.

2. Lord, I offer to you, upon your altar of atonement, all my sins and offences, which I have committed before your face and your holy Angels, from the day when first I was able to sin to this hour, so that you can burn them all together, and consume them with the fire of your love, and blot out all the stains of my sins, and purge my conscience from all wrongdoing, and restore to me your grace, which I lost by sinning, fully forgiving me for all, and mercifully receiving me for the kiss of peace.

3. What can I do about my sins, save by humbly confessing them and grieving over them, and unceasingly imploring your atoning grace? I beg you, hear me, in your mercy, when I stand before you, my God. All my sins exceedingly displease you; I have no wish ever to commit them again; but for them I grieve, and shall grieve, for as long as I shall live, prepared to do penance, and make restitution as far as in me lies. Banish my sins from me, God, banish them for the sake of your holy name; save my soul which you have redeemed by your precious Blood. Look, I commit myself to your mercy, I resign myself into your hands. Deal with me according to your goodness, not according to my wickedness and iniquity.

4. I offer to you, too, all good things which I have, few and marred though they be, that you may mend them and make them holy, that you may make them pleasing and acceptable to yourself, and always lead them on to betterment, and no

less bring me, a slothful and useless manikin, through to a blessed and praiseworthy end.

5. I also offer to you all the holy longings of the devout, the needs of parents, friends, brothers, sisters, and all my dear ones, and of those who have done me or others good for the love of you, and who have petitioned or sought for prayers to be said by me for themselves, or all near to them, whether still living in the flesh, or already dead to this world, that these all may be conscious of the help of the coming of your grace to them, the work of consolation, protection from dangers, release from pains, and that, snatched from all evils, they may joyfully render exceeding thanks to God.

6. I offer to you also prayers and the offerings of atonement, for those especially, who have in some way injured me, saddened me or reviled me, or have caused me some loss or trouble; for all those, too, whom, at times, I have saddened, disturbed, troubled or stumbled, in words or deeds, knowingly or unknowingly, that equally you may forgive all of us our sins and offences. Take from our hearts, Lord, all suspicion, wrath, anger and contention, and whatever can wound love, and diminish brotherly affection. Pity, pity, Lord, those who ask for your mercy, give grace to the needy, and make us so to live that we may be worthy fully to enjoy your grace, and go forward to eternal life. Amen.

TEN

On the Need not Lightly to Forego Holy Communion

The Voice of the Beloved

1. 'You must often hasten back to the fountain of grace and divine mercy, to the fountain of goodness and all purity, that you may be healed from your passions and vices, and deserve to be made stronger and more watchful against all the temptations and wiles of the devil. The enemy, knowing the profit and mighty remedy placed in Holy Communion, strives by all means and always, as far as he is able, to draw back and hinder the faithful and devout.'

2. 'For when some set about to make ready for Holy Communion, they suffer the worst intrusions and deceptions of Satan. The wicked spirit himself, as it is written in Job, comes among the sons of God to trouble them with his accustomed evil-doing, or to make them over-timid and puzzled, and to lessen their love, or by attacking it to take away their faith, if perhaps they may quite abandon Communion, or approach it with lukewarmness. But no heed must be given to his wiles and fantasies, however vile and shocking they may be, for all his phantasms are to be twisted back upon his own head. The wretch must be despised and held in derision, nor must Holy Communion be omitted because of his assaults and the disturbances he stirs.'

3. 'Often, too, there stands in the way an over-carefulness about the exercise of devotion, or some anxiety about making confession. Act according as wise men advise, and put aside anxiety and scruple, because it hinders the grace of God, and destroys the mind's devotion. Do not neglect Holy Communion because of some small disturbance or heaviness of spirit, but go more quickly to confess, and readily forgive the wrongs of others. If indeed, you yourself have wronged someone, humbly plead for pardon, and God will readily forgive you.'

4. 'What profit is there in delaying confession, or postponing Communion? Cleanse yourself as soon as may be, quickly spit

out the poison, hurry to receive the remedy, and you will feel better than if you should longer put it off. If today you defer it for one thing, tomorrow, perhaps, something greater will appear, and so you could long be shut off from Communion, and become more unfit for it. As quickly as you can, shake yourself free from the day's heaviness and sluggishness, for there is no profit in continuing to be anxious, to go on longer with uneasiness, and because of little daily hindrances to sever yourself from the things of God. Indeed, it is most harmful long to postpone Communion, for this commonly brings on great listlessness. Alas, the sorrow! Some, lukewarm and undisciplined, readily accept delays in confession, and for this reason want Holy Communion to be postponed, in case they be duty-bound to give themselves to greater watchfulness of self.'

5. 'Alas, what small love and devotion they have, who so lightly put off Communion! How happy is he and acceptable to God, who so lives, and guards in such purity his conscience, that he is ready and well-disposed to take Communion on any day at all, if it were possible, and without the notice of anyone. If a person abstains occasionally, because of humility, or for some legitimate hindrance, he deserves praise on the score of reverence. But if sloth has crept in, he should stir himself up, and do what he can; and the Lord will aid his desire according to his goodwill, which God especially approves.'

6. 'But when he is held back for good reason, he will still retain his goodwill, and dutiful intention of taking Communion, so will not lack the fruit of the Sacrament, for any devout person can, on any day and at any hour, come to spiritual Communion with Christ, wholesomely and without prohibition. None the less, on certain days, and at the appointed time, he should

receive sacramentally the Body of his Redeemer, with loving reverence, and seek rather the praise and honour of God, than his own comfort. For as often as he mystically communicates, and is invisibly refreshed, so often he devoutly enacts again the mystery of Christ's incarnation and passion, and is fired to love him.'

7. 'But he who does not otherwise prepare himself, except when a festival approaches, or compelling custom, will quite often be unprepared. Blessed is he who offers himself up to God for a full sacrifice, whenever he conducts or takes Communion. In celebrating, do not be too long or too hasty, but observe the good custom of those among whom you live. You must not provoke annoyance or boredom, but follow the normal course according to the institution of our forbears, and rather keep to what benefits others than your own devotion or feelings.'

ELEVEN

On the Need for the Faithful Soul for the Body of Christ and the Holy Scriptures

The Voice of the Disciple

1. O, sweetest Lord Jesus, how great is the sweetness of the devout soul feasting with you at your banquet, where no other food is set before him to eat but yourself, his only beloved one, desirable beyond all the desiring of his heart! And sweet indeed it would be to me to shed tears from the depth of my love before you, and, along with loving Magdalen, to wash your feet with them. But where is this devotion, where this plentiful flowing forth of holy tears? Surely, in your sight, and that of your holy Angels, my whole heart should burn and

weep for joy, for I have you truly present in the Sacrament, though concealed in another form.

2. For my eyes could not bear to look on you in your own divine effulgence, nor, indeed, could the whole world continue in the blaze of the glory of your majesty. In this, therefore, you consider my feebleness, in that you hide yourself away in the Sacrament. I truly possess and adore him, whom the Angels in heaven adore, but I yet, for a time, by faith, but they by sight, and without a veil. I must be content in the light of true faith, and walk in it until the day dawns of eternal light, and the shades of symbols slope away. But when that which is perfect has come, the use of Sacraments shall cease, for the Blessed, in heaven's glory, will not need sacramental remedy, for they rejoice forever in God's presence, gazing on his glory face to face, and, changed from brightness into the brightness of God unfathomable, they taste the Word of God made flesh, as it was from the beginning and remains forevermore.

3. When I remember these wondrous things, any kind of spiritual comfort becomes heavy weariness to me, because, as long as I do not see my God openly in his glory, I count everything as nothing, which I look upon and hear in the world. You are my witness, God, that nothing can console me, and nothing created give me rest, but you, my God, whom I long to look upon for ever. But this is not possible while I abide in this state of mortality. And so I must set myself to greater patience, and submit myself to you in every longing. For even your Saints, Lord, who already rejoice with you in the kingdom of the heavens, while they lived, awaited in faith and much patience the coming of your glory. What they believed, I believe; what they hoped, I hope; whither they went, I trust that, by your grace, I, too shall come. I shall walk, meanwhile, in faith, made strong by the example of the Saints. I shall have, too, the holy books for solace and a mirror held to life, and, above all these, your most holy Body, for a special remedy and refuge.

4. For, in this life, I have, I feel, two most special needs, without which this wretched life would be, for me, beyond bearing. Held in the prison of this body, I confess I need two things, food, to wit, and light. And so you have given to me in my weakness your sacred Body for the refreshment of my mind and body, and you have set your word 'as a lamp for my feet'. Without these two I could not live, for the word of God is light to my soul, and your Sacrament the bread of life. These can also be called two tables, placed on this side and that in the treasury of your holy Church. One table is that of the holy altar, holding the holy bread, that is, the precious Body of Christ. The other is that of the divine law, containing the holy doctrine, teaching the right faith, and leading through steadfastly to that which lies beyond the veil, where is the holy of holies.

5. Thanks be to you, Lord Jesus, light of eternal light, for the table of holy doctrine which you have provided for us through your servants the Prophets, the Apostles and other Teachers. Thanks be to you, Creator, and Redeemer of men, who, to make manifest your love to the whole world, have made ready a great feast, in which, not the symbolic lamb, but your own most holy Body and Blood you have set forth to be eaten, making all the faithful glad with a sacred banquet, and giving them fully to drink the cup of salvation, in which are all the delicious things of paradise, and the holy Angels feast with us, but with a happier sweetness.

6. O, how great and honourable is the office of the Priests, to whom it is given with holy words to consecrate the Lord of majesty, to bless him with the lips, to hold him with the hands, to take in their own mouth, and serve to others! O how clean must be those hands, how pure the mouth, how holy the body, how spotless will be the heart of the Priest, into which so often enters the Maker of purity. From the mouth of the Priest, who so often receives the Sacrament of Christ, nothing that is not holy, no word that is not worthy and profitable should proceed.

7. Without guile and chaste should be those eyes, which are wont to gaze on the Body of Christ. The hands should be clean and lifted towards heaven, which are wont to handle the Creator of heaven and earth. To Priests in particular it is said in the law: 'Be holy, because I your God am holy.'

8. May your grace, omnipotent God, aid us, that we who have taken up the priestly office, may have strength to wait upon you worthily and devoutly, in all purity and with a good conscience. And if we are not able to live in such innocence of life as we ought, grant us, none the less to weep, as we ought, over the sins which we have committed, and in the spirit of humility and the purpose of goodwill, to serve you more earnestly for the rest of life.

TWELVE

On the Communicant's Need for Careful Preparation

The Voice of the Beloved

1. 'I am the lover of purity and the giver of all holiness. I seek a pure heart, and there is my resting-place. Prepare for me an upper room, nobly furnished, and I will keep the Passover in your home, along with my disciples. If you wish me to come to you and to stay with you, purge out the old leaven, and make clean the small habitation of your heart. Shut out the whole world and all the turmoil of its vices; sit like a lonely sparrow on the roof, and think of your transgressions in the bitterness of your soul, for everyone who loves prepares for his lover the best and most beautiful abode, because hereby is recognised the affection of one who receives the beloved.'

2. 'Yet know that you cannot sufficiently make this preparation from the worth of your own action, though for a whole year you prepare yourself with nothing else in your mind, but it is by my faithfulness and grace alone that you are allowed to approach my table – as if a beggar should be called to a rich man's banquet, and should have nought else to give in return for his kindness, than by self-humiliation and rendering of thanks to him. Do, therefore, what in you lies, and do it with diligence, not from custom nor from obligation, but with fear, reverence and love receive the Body of your beloved Lord God, who deigns to come to you. I am he who called you; I commanded it to be done; I will make good what you lack; come and receive me.'

3. 'When I grant the grace of devotion, give thanks to your God, not because you are worthy, but because I had pity on you. If you do not have devotion, but rather feel yourself dry, persist in prayer, sigh and knock, and do not give up until you deserve to receive a crumb or drop of saving grace. You need me, I do not need you. You do not come to sanctify me, but I come to sanctify you and make you a better person. You come to be sanctified by me, and made one with me, to receive fresh grace and to be fired anew to amend your ways.

Do not neglect this grace, but with all diligence make your heart ready, and bring your beloved to yourself.'

4. 'But you must not only prepare yourself for devotion before Communion, but also carefully keep yourself in it after receiving the Sacrament. No less a watchfulness is demanded afterwards than devout preparation before, for strict watchfulness afterwards is in turn the finest preparation for acquiring greater grace. In this way, indeed, is one made most unprepared, if straightway he is too eager for consolations outside. Shun too much talking; remain apart and enjoy your God, for you have him whom the whole world cannot take from you. I am he to whom you must wholly give yourself, so that henceforth you may live, not in yourself, but in me, freed from all stress.'

THIRTEEN

On the Devout Soul's Yearning for Union with Christ in the Sacrament

The Voice of the Disciple

1. Who will grant me, Lord, to discover you alone, and open my whole heart to you, and enjoy you as my soul longs to do, and that no one may henceforth despise me, nor anything created move me or think upon me, but you alone should speak to me, and I to you, just as the lover is wont to speak to his beloved, and friend have fellowship with friend? This I pray, this I long for, that I may be wholly one with you, and withdraw my heart from all created things, and, through Holy Communion and its frequent celebration, learn better to savour the heavenly and the eternal. Ah, Lord God, when shall I be wholly united and lost in you, and utterly forgetful

of myself? 'You in me and I in you'; so grant that thus we may abide together in one.

2. Truly, you are my beloved, chosen from thousands, in whom it has pleased my soul to dwell all the days of its life. Truly you are my peacemaker, in whom is perfect peace and true rest, and apart from whom is toil and grief and misery unbounded. You are, in truth, a God who hides himself, and your counsel is not with the ungodly, but your speech is with the humble and sincere. O, how sweet, Lord, is your spirit which, that you may show your sweetness towards your children, deigns to refresh them with that bread most sweet that comes down from heaven. Truly there is no other nation so great that has gods which draw close to it, as you, our God, are at hand with your faithful ones to whom, to comfort them each day, and lift heavenwards their heart, you give yourself to feed them and delight.

3. For what other nation is there so renowned as the common people of Christ, or what created under heaven so beloved as the devout soul, whom God approaches that he may feed it with his glorious flesh. O, grace unspeakable, O wondrous condescension, O love beyond measure, uniquely bestowed upon men! But what shall I return to the Lord for that grace, for love so excellent? There is nothing that I can give more acceptably than my heart in tribute totally to God for closest union with him. Then all that is within me shall make glad, when my soul shall be made perfectly one with God. Then will he say to me: 'If you will be with me, I will be with you.' And I will reply to him: 'Deign, Lord, to abide with me, and I will gladly be with you. This is all my longing, that my heart be joined with you.'

On the Ardent Longing of Some for the Body of Christ

The Voice of the Disciple

1. O, how great is the abundance of your sweetness, Lord, which you have laid up for those who fear you. When I remember some devout persons before your Sacrament, Lord, drawing near with the greatest devotion and love, then too often I am dismayed in heart and blush that I approach the altar and the table of Holy Communion so lukewarm in heart, yea, cold, that I stay so dry and without heartfelt emotion, that I am not wholly on fire in your presence, my God, nor so passionately drawn near and affected, as many devout ones have been, that from their great longing for Communion, and the heart's love which they felt, have been unable to hold back from tears, but with the mouth of heart and body equally, panted deep within for you, God, the living spring, powerless to control or satisfy their hunger unless they should receive your Body with all joyfulness and eagerness of the spirit.

2. O, their truly ardent faith providing a visible and convincing argument that you are there! For they truly recognise their Lord 'in the breaking of bread', whose heart so strongly 'burns within them', from Jesus' walking with them. For (alas, the sorrow!) such love and such devotion often is far from me, such mighty love and ardour. Be merciful to me, good Jesus, sweet and kind, and grant to your poor supplicant, at least sometimes to experience in Holy Communion a little of your heartmoving love, that my faith may grow strong, hope in your goodness increase, and that love, once thoroughly afire, and having known heaven's manna, may never die down.

3. But your mercy is strong, even to supply me with the grace I long for, and, when the day of your good pleasure shall come, to visit me in your exceeding mercy, with the spirit of fervour. And, indeed, although I do not burn with longing as great as that of your most specially devout ones, yet, by your grace, I have a longing for that longing aflame, longing, I say, to be made a partner of all such fervent lovers of yourself, and to be numbered in their holy company.

FIFTEEN

On the Winning of Grace and Devotion by Humility and Self-abnegation

The Voice of the Beloved

1. 'You should seek earnestly the grace of devotion, look for it with longing, wait for it with patience and with confidence, receive it gratefully, hold fast to it humbly, work with it zealously, and leave to God the time and manner of heaven's visitation until it come to pass. Chiefly, you must humble yourself, when you are conscious in your heart of small devotion or none, but not to be cast down or beyond measure saddened. God often gives in one brief moment that which he has for a long time denied. In the end he sometimes gives what he deferred when first you prayed for it.'

2. 'If grace were always quickly given, and were attendant on your prayer, a weak man would not be able well to bear it. That is why the grace of devotion must be awaited in good hope and humble patience. Nevertheless put it down to yourself and to your sins, when it is not given or even secretly taken away. It is sometimes a trifle which hinders or hides grace, if indeed it should be called a trifle, and not rather an enormity which impedes such a blessing. But if you shall remove that very thing, small though it be or great, and completely conquer it, it will be as you have sought.'

3. 'For immediately you have given yourself to God with all your heart, and sought neither this thing nor that according to your own will or pleasure, but have completely placed yourself in his hands, you will find yourself at unity and peace, for nothing will give you such relish and delight as the good pleasure of God's will. Whoever, therefore, shall lift his purpose up to God with singleness of heart, and shall have emptied himself of all undisciplined love, or dislike of any created thing, will be most fit to receive grace and be worthy of the gift of devotion. For God there bestows his benediction where he finds an empty vessel, and the more completely a man renounces things below, and the more, in contempt of self, he dies to self, so the more quickly grace comes, enters abundantly and lifts higher the free heart.'

4. 'Then shall he see, and overflow, and wonder, and his heart shall be enlarged within him, because the hand of the Lord is with him, and in his hand he has wholly placed himself for evermore. Look, so shall a man be blessed who seeks God with his whole heart, nor receives his soul in vain. This man, in receiving the Holy Eucharist, wins the great grace of union with God, because he has no regard to his own devotion and consolation, but, beyond all devotion and consolation, looks to the glory and honour of God.'

On Exposing our Needs to Christ and Imploring his Grace

The Voice of the Disciple

1. O, most sweet and loving Lord, whom I now long devoutly to receive, you know my weakness, and the need which I suffer, in what evils and sins I lie, how often I am burdened, tempted, disturbed and soiled. For remedy I come to you, I beg you for comfort and relief. I speak to one who knows all things, to whom all that is within me is laid bare, and who alone can perfectly console and aid me. You know of what blessings I chiefly stand in need, and how poor I am in virtues.

2. Look, I stand before you poor and naked, begging for grace and imploring mercy. Refresh your hungry supplicant, kindle my coldness with the fire of your love, lighten my blindness with the brightness of your presence. Turn all earthly things to bitterness for me, all burdensome and adverse things to patience, all feeble and created things into contempt and forgetfulness. Lift up my heart to you in heaven, and dismiss me not to wander through the earth. Do you alone be sweet to me from this day for evermore, because you alone are my food and drink, my love and joy, my sweetness and all my good.

3. Would that, by your presence you would set me all on fire, burn me up and change me into yourself, so that I may become one spirit with you by the grace of inner union, and the melting of burning love! Suffer me not to go away from you hungry and dry, but deal with me in mercy as you have often dealt wondrously with your Saints. What a wonder if I should be wholly set on fire from you, and in my self should pass away, since you are always burning fire and never pass away, love that makes the heart pure, and lightens the understanding.

On the Burning Heart and the Passionate Longing to Receive Christ

The Voice of the Disciple

1. With the deepest devotion and burning love, with the whole heart's fervour and feeling, I long, Lord, to receive you, in the same manner as many Saints and devout people, have longed for you in taking Communion, you whom they have most pleased in sanctity of life, dwelling in all fervent devotion. O, my God, eternal love, my whole good, happiness without end, I desire to receive you with longing most passionate, with reverence most fitting, such as any of the Saints ever had or could experience.

2. And though I am unworthy to entertain all those feelings of devotion, yet I offer to you all the affection of my heart, as if I were the only one to have those most welcome, flaming, hot desires. But whatever a holy mind can conceive and long for, these all, with deepest worship and heartfelt fervour, I present and offer to you. I desire to hold back nothing for myself, but willingly and gladly make a sacrifice to you of myself and all I have. Lord, my God, my creator, my redeemer, with such love, reverence, praise and honour, with such gratitude, worthiness and love, with such faith, hope and purity, I strive to receive you today, as your most holy mother, the glorious Virgin Mary, received and longed for you, when to the Angel bringing the good news to her of the mystery of the incarnation, she humbly and devoutly replied: 'Look, the handmaid of the Lord, let it be to me according to your word.'

3. And just as your blessed forerunner, most excellent of Saints, John the Baptiser, joyous at your presence, leaped in the Holy Spirit's gladness, while still shut in his mother's womb, and later, seeing Jesus walking among men, deeply humbling himself with devout love, said: 'But the friend of the bridegroom, who stands and hears him, rejoices greatly because of the bridegroom's voice,' so I, too, with great and holy longings, pray to be set on fire, and offer myself to you with my whole heart. So also I offer and present to you, the loud joys of all devout hearts, their ecstasies of mind, insights beyond nature and heavenly visions, along with all virtues and praises proclaimed by every creature in heaven and on earth, and yet to be proclaimed, for me, and all commended to me in prayer, that by all of them you may be worthily praised, and glorified forever.

4. Accept my prayers, Lord my God, and my longings to render praises without end, and unbounded benediction, which are justly due to you, according to the vastness of your greatness, which is beyond describing. These I render to you, and long still to render each passing day and moment of time, and to render to you, along with me, thanks and praises, I invite and call upon, with supplications and all expressions of love, all the spirits of heaven and all your faithful ones.

5. Let all peoples, tribes and tongues praise you and your holy and honeyflowing name, and magnify you with loftiest jubilation and burning devotion. And whoever with reverence and devotion celebrates your most high Sacrament, and receives it in full faith, may they be counted worthy in your sight to receive grace and mercy, and let them for me, a sinner, pray with supplication. And when they have won the devotion they desire and joyous union, are truly comforted, and wondrously refreshed and are departed from your holy heavenly table, let them deign to remember poor me.

On Approaching Christ's Sacrament Simply as an Humble Imitator of Christ Subjecting Reason to a Holy Faith

The Voice of the Beloved

1. 'You must beware of an inquisitive and useless prying into this most deep Sacrament, if you do not want to be plunged into the abyss of doubting. He who looks into grandeur, shall be overwhelmed by its glory. God can work more than man can understand. A reverent and humble enquiry into truth can be borne, if it is ever ready to be instructed, zealous to walk according to the wholesome opinions of the Fathers.'

2. 'Blessed is the simplicity which abandons the hard paths of questionings, and travels along the plain, sure tracks of God's commandments. Many have lost devotion in the desire to pry into higher matters. Faith is what is asked of you, and an honest life, not loftiness of intellect, nor deep knowledge of God's mysteries. If you do not understand or grasp what lies beneath you, in what way will you comprehend what is above? Surrender to God, and subdue your sense to faith, and the light of knowledge will be given you, as shall be useful and needful to you.'

3. 'Some are grievously tempted in the matter of faith and the Sacrament, but this is not to be set down against them, but rather to the enemy. Do not be anxious, nor argue with your own thoughts, nor reply to the doubtings which the devil injects, but believe what God says, believe his Saints and Prophets, and the wicked foe will fly from you. It is often of profit for God's servant to endure such things, for the devil does not tempt unbelievers and sinners whom he already holds with certainty, but he tempts and harries the faithful and devout in many ways.'

4. 'Press on, therefore, with simple and undoubting faith, and with prayerful reverence approach the Sacrament. And whatever you cannot understand, commit, without anxiety, to God omnipotent. God does not disappoint you; he is disappointed who trusts too much in himself. God walks with the simple, reveals himself to the humble, gives understanding to the little ones, makes meaning clear to pure minds, and hides his grace from the inquisitive and proud. Human reason is weak and can be deceived, but true faith cannot be deceived.'

5. 'All reason and natural investigation must follow faith, not go ahead of it or break it, for faith and love there most excel, and work in hidden ways in this most holy Sacrament beyond all excellence. God, eternal, immeasurable, and of boundless power, does great things, beyond all searching, in heaven and on earth, and his wondrous works cannot be traced out. If such were the works of God that they could be easily grasped by human reason, they would not be called wonderful or unspeakable.'

HODDER CLASSICS
Classic Christian writing for today

As a company with Christian roots, Hodder
& Stoughton has a rich publishing heritage.
Hodder Faith is proud to have on its list a
series of classics that have inspired believers
from all traditions over the years.

Each book in the Hodder Classics series is a
devotional or theological work that has been
a key influence in the life of the Church, and
in keeping these titles in print, we hope to
continue a tradition of making available
and accessible the work of important
Christian thinkers.